The **SSAT** Course Book

MIDDLE & UPPER LEVEL

QUANTITATIVE

SUMMIT EDUCATIONAL GROUP

Focusing on the Individual Student

Copyright Statement

The SSAT Course Book, along with all Summit Educational Group Course Materials, is protected by copyright. Under no circumstances may any Summit materials be reproduced, distributed, published, or licensed by any means.

Summit Educational Group reserves the right to refuse to sell materials to any individual, school, district, or organization that fails to comply with our copyright policies.

Third party materials used to supplement Summit Course Materials are subject to copyright protection vested in their respective publishers. These materials are likewise not reproducible under any circumstances.

Ownership of Trademarks

Summit Educational Group is the owner of the trademarks "Summit Educational Group" and the pictured Summit logo, as well as other marks that the Company may seek to use and protect from time to time in the ordinary course of business.

SSAT is a trademark of the Enrollment Management Association.

All other trademarks referenced are the property of their respective owners.

CONTENTS

TEST-TAKING FUNDAMENTALS

About the SSAT   2
SSAT Structure   3
Scoring   4
Knowing Your Limits   5
Setting Your Quantitative Goal & Range   6
Beating the SSAT   8
Making Your Best Guess   10
Using the Answer Choices   12
General Tactics   14

QUANTITATIVE

General Information   18
Plugging In   20
Solving Backwards   22
Choosing Numbers   24
Math Tips   26
Chapter Review   27

NUMBER CONCEPTS & OPERATIONS

Vocabulary   31
Addition, Subtraction, Multiplication, & Division   32
Odd & Even Integers   36
Positive & Negative Numbers   38
Divisibility & Remainders   40
Multiples & Factors   42
Fractions   46
Reducing Fractions   50
Adding & Subtracting Fractions   54
Multiplying & Dividing Fractions   58
Place Value   64
Rounding & Estimation   66
Decimals   70
Percent-Decimal-Fraction Conversion   72
Percents   76

Ratios   82
Proportions   86
Order of Operations   90
Sequences, Patterns, & Logic   92
Chapter Review   98
Arithmetic Practice   100
Arithmetic Middle Level Practice   114
Arithmetic Upper Level Practice   128

ALGEBRA

Vocabulary   145
Absolute Value   146
Scientific Notation   148
Exponents   150
Multiplying & Dividing Numbers with Exponents   152
Roots   154
Algebraic Expressions   158
Algebraic Equations   162
Inequalities   166
Simultaneous Equations   170
Translating   174
Functions   178
SSAT Functions   180
Quadratic Equations   184
Chapter Review   188
Algebra Practice   190
Algebra Middle Level Practice   200
Algebra Upper Level Practice   206

GEOMETRY

Vocabulary   215
Angles   216
Parallel Lines   220
Isosceles & Equilateral Triangles   222
Right Triangles   224
Area & Perimeter – Rectangle & Square   228
Area & Perimeter – Triangle   232
Circles   236

Volume   240
Spatial Reasoning   242
Coordinate Plane   246
Midpoint & Distance   248
Transformation   250
Slope   252
Graphing Lines   254
Chapter Review   260
Geometry Practice   262
Geometry Middle Level Practice   272
Geometry Upper Level Practice   282

DATA ANALYSIS & PROBABILITY

Averages   294
Median, Mode, & Range   298
Sets   300
Counting   302
Probability   304
Interpreting Data   308
Chapter Review   314
Data Analysis & Probability Practice   316
Data Analysis & Probability Middle Level Practice   320
Data Analysis & Probability Upper Level Practice   324

ANSWER KEY

Number Concepts & Operations
Number Concepts & Operations Practice
Algebra
Algebra Practice
Geometry
Geometry Practice
Data Analysis & Probability
Data Analysis & Probability Practice

Preface

Since 1988, when two Yale University graduates started Summit Educational Group, tens of thousands of students have benefited from Summit's innovative, comprehensive, and highly effective test preparation. You will too.

Successful test-takers not only possess the necessary academic skills but also understand how to take the SSAT. Through your SSAT program, you'll learn both. You'll review and develop the academic skills you need, and you'll learn practical, powerful and up-to-date test-taking strategies.

The *Summit SSAT Course Book* provides the skills, strategies, and practice necessary for success on the SSAT. The result of much research and revision, the book is the most effective, innovative and comprehensive preparation tool available.

The book's first chapter – Test-Taking Fundamentals – gives students a solid foundation of SSAT information and general test-taking strategies. Some of the more important topics covered include question difficulty, scoring, and avoiding attractors.

The next chapters correspond to the main content areas of the SSAT Quantitative sections. Each chapter is divided into manageable topic modules. Modules consist of the skills, strategies, and common question types for particular topics, several *Try It Out* questions, and several *Put It Together* questions. The questions progress in order of difficulty. At the end of each chapter, homework questions provide additional practice.

We are confident that you will not find a more complete or effective SSAT program anywhere.

We value your feedback and are always striving to improve our materials. Please write to us with comments, questions, or suggestions for future editions at:

      edits@mytutor.com

Your program will give you the skills, knowledge, and confidence you need to score your best.

Good luck, and have fun!

Chapter Summaries

We've reproduced the Chapter Summaries below to give you a preview of what you'll be covering. The Summaries are meant to serve as quick, condensed reference guides to the most important concepts. Obviously, you can't bring them into the test with you, but from now up until the night before the test, use them to preview and review the material covered in this book. Of course, Chapter Summaries also reside at the end of each chapter.

General Test-Taking Summary

❑ Your SSAT preparation will focus on learning strategies and strengthening core skills.

Your responsibilities include doing 1-2 hours of homework per session and learning as much vocabulary as you can.

❑ Know your limits. Put your time and energy into the problems you are most capable of answering. If you struggle with difficult problems or with finishing sections in time, spend more of your time on the easy and medium problems and less time on the difficult problems.

❑ Never leave an easy problem blank. On an easy problem, an answer that instinctively seems right usually is.

❑ Avoid attractors. The test writers predict potential mistakes by students and include those mistakes as answer choices.

❑ If you can certainly eliminate at least two answers, you should guess from the remaining answer choices. The more answers you can eliminate, the greater advantage you have.

❑ On a multiple-choice test, the answer choices can provide you with further ammunition to solve the problem. Don't get stuck trying to find an answer with a certain method. If you can't solve the problem in the forward direction, try to solve in the reverse direction by using the answer choices.

Quantitative

❑ Format/Directions

Questions get harder as you go. The last question in a Quantitative section is much more difficult and takes much longer to solve than the first question, but they are both worth just one point. Pace yourself; work patiently and carefully.

❑ Plugging In

Use answer choices to help you solve problems.

When plugging in, start with answer choice (C).

❑ Solving Backwards

Consider what information the question asks for and think of what you must do to find that information.

Answer choices can sometimes be clues for what type of answer you should get.

❑ Choosing Numbers

In complex equations or word problems, choose values for variables or unknown numbers. This can make abstract problems easier to handle.

Number Concepts & Operations

❑ Addition, Subtraction, Multiplication, & Division

On SSAT math problems, you will have to calculate sums, differences, products, and quotients.

❑ Odd & Even Integers

An odd number is an integer that is not divisible by 2. An even number is an integer that is divisible by 2.

❑ Positive & Negative Numbers

A positive number is any number that is greater than 0. A negative number is any number that is less than 0.

❑ Divisibility & Remainders

A number is divisible by another number if it can be evenly divided by that number with no remainder. When a number does not divide evenly into another number, the number that remains at the end of the division is called the remainder.

❑ Multiples & Factors

A multiple is the product of a particular number and another number. A factor of a number is a number that divides evenly into that number.

❑ Fractions

Fractions are used to represent portions of a whole. Fractions are written as $\dfrac{PART}{WHOLE}$.

To add or subtract fractions, first adjust the fractions so they have a common denominator. To multiply fractions, multiply straight across.

Two numbers are reciprocals if their product is 1. To find the reciprocal of a fraction, "flip" the fraction by switching its numerator and denominator.

❑ Place Value

Decimals are a way of writing fractions whose denominators are powers of 10. The position of each digit in a number determines the digit's place value.

❑ Rounding & Estimation

To round a number, look at the digit to the right of the place you're rounding to. If that digit is greater than or equal to 5, round up; if that digit is less than 5, round down.

❑ Percents

"Is over of" calls for a proportion. One side of the proportion is the percentage written as a fraction. The other side is a fraction in which the numerator is the number that comes after the word "is" and the denominator is the number that comes after the word "of."

❑ Ratios

When two quantities are compared by dividing one quantity by the other, the comparison is called a ratio. A ratio may be written as "X:Y" or "X/Y" or "X to Y."

❑ Proportions

A proportion is a statement that two ratios are equivalent. The quickest way to solve proportions is usually to cross-multiply. With both ratios written as fractions, multiply the numerator of each ratio by the denominator of the other, and set the products equal to each other. In other words, $\frac{a}{b} = \frac{c}{d}$ is a proportion if $ad = bc$.

❑ Order of Operations

To simplify a problem with multiple operations, you need to follow the order of operations.

1. Parentheses: ( )
2. Exponents: 3^2
3. Multiplication: 2×4
4. Division: $6 \div 2$
5. Addition: $5 + 6$
6. Subtraction: $9 - 6$

❑ Sequences, Patterns, & Logic

To compare the relative sizes of decimals, line up the decimal points. To compare the relative sizes of fractions, find the lowest common denominator and compare the numerators. Consecutive numbers are whole numbers that increase or decrease incrementally by 1. Sequences and patterns can often be solved by recognizing trends or by writing out the numbers.

Algebra

❑ Absolute Value

The absolute value of a number is the distance between the number and zero on the number line. Think of the absolute value of a number as the "positive value" of that number. To simplify an expression within an absolute value sign, simplify just as you would simplify an expression in parentheses. Then take the absolute value of the result.

❑ Scientific Notation

In "scientific notation," a number is written so that the largest digit is in the units place, and it is multiplied by a power of 10.

❑ Exponents

An exponent tells you how many times to multiply a number by itself. To multiply two numbers with the same base, add the exponents. To divide two numbers with the same base, subtract the exponents. To raise a power to a power, multiply the exponents.

❑ Roots

A square root (also known as a radical) is an exponent of 2 in reverse. A number's square root is the number which, when multiplied by itself, gives you the original number.

❑ Algebraic Expressions

Simplifying an algebraic expression is often the first step in solving an algebraic equation. To simplify an algebraic expression, combine similar terms. Use the distributive property to multiply a single term by an expression inside parentheses. When multiplying two binomials, each term must be multiplied by each term in the other binomial. Use the FOIL method: multiply the first terms, outside terms, inside terms, and last terms.

❑ Algebraic Equations

To solve an equation, get the variable by itself on one side of the equal sign. Keep the equation balanced. If you do something to one side, such as add a number or divide by a number, you must do the same to the other side. To solve an equation with a fraction, first get rid of the fraction by multiplying both sides of the equation by the denominator. To solve an equation with a radical sign, first get rid of the radical sign by isolating the radical on one side of the equation and then squaring both sides.

❑ Simultaneous Equations

Elimination Method – Add or subtract equations to cancel one of the variables and solve for the other. You may have to multiply an equation by some number to eliminate a variable before the equations are added or subtracted.

Substitution Method – Solve one equation for one of the variables, and then substitute that value for that variable in the other equation.

❑ Translating

Transforming words into mathematical equations is the first step in solving many SSAT problems. It is especially helpful in solving word problems. After reading the question, state in your own words what the problem is asking you to find. Break the problem into its parts and make certain you understand each of them. Translate the parts into "math language," and use the math equations you have set up to get the answer.

❑ Functions

A function is an "instruction" or "process" that for any value of x you put in will give you a single value of y (or $f(x)$) as a result. You can think of a function as a machine that takes inputs and converts them to outputs. You input a value for x, and the machine puts out a value for $f(x)$. To evaluate a function, $f(x)$, for a particular value of x, simply substitute that value everywhere you see an x.

❑ SSAT Functions

On SSAT function problems, you will be asked to solve an equation using an unfamiliar symbol. The symbol represents the mathematical function to be carried out.

❑ Quadratic Equations

Factoring is expanding in reverse. Find common factors among the terms in an expression and rewrite using multiplication. Solve quadratic equations by following four simple steps:

1. Set the equation equal to zero.
2. Factor the equation.
3. Set each factor equal to zero.
4. Solve each of the resulting equations.

Geometry

❑ Angles

A 90° angle is called a right angle. The measure of a straight line is equal to 180°. Guesstimate angles on figures that are drawn to scale.

❑ Parallel Lines

When two lines intersect, the angles opposite each other are called vertical angles. Vertical angles are equal.

❑ Isosceles and Equilateral Triangles

An isosceles triangle is any triangle that has two equal sides. In addition, the angles opposite the congruent sides are equal. An equilateral triangle is a triangle that has all three sides equal. In addition, all angles are 60°.

❑ Right Triangles

A right triangle is any triangle that has a 90° angle as one of its angles. The Pythagorean Theorem states that in any right triangle the square of the hypotenuse is equal to the sum of the squares of the other two sides.

❑ Area and Perimeter – Rectangle and Square

Perimeter is the distance around the edge of a two-dimensional figure. Area is the measurement of the space inside a two-dimensional figure. Area is measured in square units. A rectangle is a 4-sided figure with 4 right angles. In a rectangle, opposite sides are equal. A square is a rectangle that has 4 equal sides.

❑ Area and Perimeter – Triangle

To find the perimeter of a triangle, add the lengths of all of the sides. To find the area of a triangle, use the following formula: $A = \frac{1}{2}bh$, where A = area, b = base, and h = height.

❑ Circles

Circumference is the distance around the edge of the circle. Circumference = $2 \times \pi \times r$

The area of a circle is found using the formula: Area = $\pi \times r^2$

❑ Volume

Volume is the space occupied by a three-dimensional figure. Volume of a cube: $V = s^3$
Volume of a rectangular box: $V = l \times w \times h$

❑ Spatial Reasoning

Spatial reasoning questions test your problem-solving skills and your ability to visualize 2-dimensional and 3-dimensional situations. During the test, use anything available to help solve spatial reasoning questions.

❑ Midpoint & Distance

The midpoint of a line segment is the point exactly in the middle between two end points. To find the midpoint, calculate the average of the x-coordinates and the average of the y-coordinates.

Distance between points (x_1, y_1) and (x_2, y_2), $= \sqrt{(x_2 - x_1)^2 + (y_2 - y_1)^2}$

❑ Transformations

Translation is the process of moving a point or figure a specified distance in a certain direction. Reflection is the process of moving a point or figure by mirroring it over a line. Rotation is the process of moving a point or figure by rotating it around a point – often the origin. Shapes have symmetry when they can be transformed to be exactly like one another. An axis of symmetry is a line that divides a figure into symmetrical images.

❑ Slope

The slope is the amount a line moves vertically for every unit the line moves horizontally.

Use $\dfrac{\text{rise}}{\text{run}}$ to calculate slope. The slopes of perpendicular lines are negative reciprocals of each other. Parallel lines have equal slopes. Vertical lines have undefined slope, or infinite slope. Horizontal lines have slope = 0.

❑ Graphing Lines

Slope-intercept form: $y = mx + b$. In this equation, m is the slope of the line and b is the y-intercept (the point where the line crosses the y-axis and $x = 0$).

Data Analysis & Probability

❑ Averages

To find the average of a list of numbers, find the sum of the numbers and divide by the number of terms. Average = $\dfrac{\text{sum of parts}}{\text{number of parts}}$

❑ Median, Mode, & Range

The median of a set of numbers is the middle value when all the terms are listed in order according to size. The mode of a set of numbers is the number that occurs most frequently. The range is the difference between the least and greatest values in a set.

❑ Sets

A set is a collection of distinct objects, such as a group of numbers or people. Sets overlap when they have elements in common. Venn diagrams can be used to represent which elements are included in both sets.

❑ Counting

Counting problems involve calculating the total number of choices or outcomes for a situation. Formulas can be used to solve these problems, but many of these problems can also be solved with brute force, listing all of the possibilities and simply counting them.

To determine the total number of different possibilities for a certain situation, multiply the different numbers of possibilities. If there are x options for one choice, and y options for another choice, then there are $x \times y$ combinations of options available.

In permutations, the order of events matters. Use the following notations when choosing r items from a set of n items: $P(n, r)$ or $_nP_r$ or $\dfrac{n!}{(n-r)!}$

❑ Probability

Probability of an event happening = $\dfrac{\text{\# of ways the event can happen}}{\text{\# of possible outcomes}}$

To find the probability of one event *or* another event occurring, *add* the probabilities of each event. If there is any overlap between the two events, subtract this overlap from the sum.

To find the probability of one event *and* another event occurring, *multiply* the probabilities of each event.

❑ Interpreting Data

Before looking at a chart or graph question, take a moment to interpret the information presented. Note the title, labels, and units used in graphs and charts. Pay attention to the scale on line graphs and bar graphs, because they might not begin at zero.

Check your answer by reviewing the chart or graph. The figure can help you visualize the information to make sure that your answer makes sense.

Assessment and Objectives Worksheet

Complete this worksheet after the first session and refer back to it often. Amend it as necessary. It should act as a guide for how you and your tutor approach the program as a whole and how your sessions are structured.

Please be honest and open when answering the questions.

Student's Self-Assessment and Parent Assessment

- How do you feel about taking standardized tests? Consider your confidence and anxiety levels.

- Work through Table of Contents or the Chapter Reviews. Are there particular areas that stand out as areas for development?

- Other Concerns

Diagnostic Test Assessment

- Pacing

  o Did you run out of time on any or all sections? Did you feel rushed? Look for skipped questions or wrong answers toward the end of sections.

  o How will the concept of Setting Your Goal help you?

- Carelessness

  o Do you feel that carelessness is an issue? Look for wrong answers on easy questions.

  o Why do you think you make careless mistakes? Rushing? Not checking? Not reading the question carefully? Knowing "why" will allow you to attack the problem.

- Are certain areas for development evident from the diagnostic? Work through the questions you got wrong to further identify areas that might require attention.

Program Objectives

Consider your assessment, and define your objectives. Make your objectives concrete and achievable.

Objective*	How to Achieve the Objective

*Sample Objectives

Objective	How to Achieve the Objective
Reduce carelessness by 75%.	Before starting to work on a question, repeat exactly what the question is asking.
Reduce test anxiety.	Build confidence and create a detailed testing plan. Start with easier questions to build confidence and slowly build toward more challenging questions. Take pride in successes and continue to reach for goals. Try to relax.
Use Choosing Numbers and Plugging In fluently.	Tutor will point out all questions that are susceptible to these strategies. Note when a math question is susceptible to one or the other strategies.
Get excited about the test prep.	Stay positive. Know that score goals can be achieved. Learn tricks to beat the test. Make the test like a game. Focus on progress.

SUMMIT
EDUCATIONAL
GROUP

Test-Taking Fundamentals

❑ About the SSAT   2

❑ Your Responsibilities   2

❑ SSAT Structure   3

❑ Scoring   4

❑ Knowing Your Limits   5

❑ Setting Your Quantitative Goal   6

❑ Beating the SSAT   8

❑ Making Your Best Guess   10

❑ Using the Answer Choices   12

❑ General Tactics   14

About the SSAT

❑ The SSAT is used to determine acceptance into private or independent schools. The test is designed to measure students' academic potential and skills in relation to the rest of the private and independent school applicants. Because this group of test-takers is especially competitive and skilled, the test is designed to be highly challenging.

A student's performance on the SSAT is <u>not</u> designed to reflect the scores on typical school exams or grades.

The importance of this test is determined by each school's admission policies, so it is important to talk to your prospective schools as you plan your SSAT preparation.

❑ The SSAT is a "power" test, which means that its difficulty stems from how challenging its questions are rather than the challenge of a strict time constraint. Most students are able to move quickly enough to answer most of the questions on the SSAT, but the test has many tricks and traps to challenge them.

Over the course of this program, you are going to learn to recognize and overcome the SSAT's tricks and traps. You will master the SSAT by developing your test-taking abilities, working on fundamental SSAT skills, and practicing on real test questions.

❑ The SSAT is administered in two levels: the Middle Level and the Upper Level. Students who are currently in grades 5 through 7 take the Middle Level test, and students who are currently in grades 8 through 11 take the Upper Level test.

Your Responsibilities

❑ You will have about 1-2 hours of homework each session. You are expected to complete every assignment. Remember, your hard work will result in a higher score!

❑ Your scores on the verbal and reading portions of the test are determined in large part by your vocabulary and reading skill. Use flash cards, study the word groups, and read, read, read! The more you read and the more vocabulary you learn, the higher your score will be.

SSAT Structure

Writing Sample – 25 minutes

Quantitative – 30 minutes

													MATHEMATICS											
1	2	3	4	5	6	7	8	9	10	11	12	13	14	15	16	17	18	19	20	21	22	23	24	25
		EASY				→					MEDIUM				→				DIFFICULT					

Reading Comprehension – 40 minutes

															READING PASSAGES																							
1	2	3	4	5	6	7	8	9	10	11	12	13	14	15	16	17	18	19	20	21	22	23	24	25	26	27	28	29	30	31	32	33	34	35	36	37	38	39	40
													NOT IN ORDER OF DIFFICULTY																										

Verbal – 30 minutes

														SYNONYMS															
1	2	3	4	5	6	7	8	9	10	11	12	13	14	15	16	17	18	19	20	21	22	23	24	25	26	27	28	29	30
		EASY				→					MEDIUM				→				DIFFICULT										

														ANALOGIES															
31	32	33	34	35	36	37	38	39	40	41	42	43	44	45	46	47	48	49	50	51	52	53	54	55	56	57	58	59	60
		EASY				→					MEDIUM				→				DIFFICULT										

Quantitative – 30 minutes

													MATHEMATICS											
1	2	3	4	5	6	7	8	9	10	11	12	13	14	15	16	17	18	19	20	21	22	23	24	25
		EASY				→					MEDIUM				→				DIFFICULT					

❑ An official SSAT contains an additional section, not shown above, known as the "Experimental Section." This is used as a trial for new test questions, and your results are <u>not</u> used to calculate your score.

The Experimental Section contains 16 questions and is 15 minutes long. It can contain any type of question from the SSAT.

Scoring

❏ The SSAT scoring method is a complex system that is designed to best reflect each student's standing within the very competitive group of SSAT students.

❏ **Every question on the SSAT is worth one raw score point**. Therefore, the easiest question is worth just as much as the most difficult question. There are no points for skipped questions. Each incorrect answer results in a ¼ point deduction from the points that have been earned. **The total number of correct answers, minus the total penalty for incorrect answers, is the *raw score*.**

❏ Your raw score is converted to a *scaled score* for each section. **The raw score for each SSAT section is scaled to adjust for varying difficulty among the different editions of the test**. The SSAT is scaled on a bell curve so that the majority of students achieve middling scores.

For the Upper Level test, the scaled score for each section falls between 500 and 800. For the Middle Level test, the scaled score falls between 440 and 710. You will also receive a total scaled score, which is the sum of the section scores.

❏ You will receive percentile scores for each section that tell how you performed with respect to other students in your grade. For example, a score of 55 means you did as well as or better than 55% of students who also took the SSAT. Your percentile score ranks you among all students who have taken the test in your grade over the past three years. In general, your **percentile is the most important score**.

Your percentile might seem quite low because you are being compared to other students applying to independent schools, which is a very competitive and well-educated group. Within this group, achieving a high rank requires a great level of skill and preparation.

❏ Your writing sample is not scored, but is sent directly to the admissions committees of the schools to which you apply. Many schools consider your writing skills as a factor for admission and may want to see how well you write under test conditions.

Knowing Your Limits

❑ Put your time and energy into the problems you are most capable of answering. If you struggle with difficult problems or with finishing sections in time, spend more of your time on the easy and medium problems and less time on the difficult problems. Here's why:

- Because your percentile scores reflect your <u>grade level</u> performance, you may not need to answer every question to score well. If you are at the lower end of the grade spectrum, this means you may be able to omit several questions and still score well.

- You'll minimize mistakes on difficult questions, which often contain attractor or trap answers.

- You'll be less hurried, and you'll make fewer careless mistakes.

❑ Push your limits.

As you prepare for the SSAT, try to learn from the questions that give you trouble. Note your mistakes and make sure that you don't repeat them. Pay attention to the questions that are the most difficult and note what makes them so challenging and how to solve them.

As your skills improve, you will be able to answer more and more of the questions on the SSAT. You will learn to recognize tricks and traps and work with more speed and confidence.

Setting Your Quantitative Goal

❑ Using your diagnostic results and previous test scores, set a realistic score goal.

❑ Unlike a school test where you might need to get 90% of the questions right to get a good score, you might need only 60% to reach your score goal on the SSAT.

❑ The following conversion tables are based on data for 8th grade students taking the Upper Level SSAT. Note that the scoring scale can vary significantly between different SSAT tests. Therefore, these conversion tables cannot always be accurate.

QUANTITATIVE SCORE CONVERSION		
Raw Score	Scaled Score	Percentile Rank
15	640	31
16	648	35
17	656	39
18	661	42
19	665	44
20	667	46
21	676	50
22	683	54
23	687	56
24	690	58
25	692	60
26	698	63
27	704	66
28	708	69
29	713	71
30	716	73
31	725	77
32	730	79
33	734	81
34	738	82
35	740	84
36	747	86
37	752	88
38	755	89
39	759	90
40	764	91
41	767	92
42	770	93
43	777	94
44	784	95
45	790	96

Setting Your Quantitative Range

❏ Your range is the number of questions you need to attempt in order to achieve your goal.

For many students, answering every problem on the SSAT will prevent them from scoring to their potential. Attempting every question on the SSAT means you'll have to rush (which can lead to careless mistakes) and you'll make mistakes on difficult questions. Because of the penalty for incorrect answers, you should know your limits and stay within your range.

❏ Use the Goal and Range tables below to determine your approximate range for each section

QUANTITATIVE GOAL & RANGE			
Raw Goal	Questions to Attempt	Questions You Can Skip	Questions You Can Miss
15	31	19	13
20	35	15	12
25	39	11	11
30	42	8	10
35	45	5	8
40	47	3	6
45	49	1	3
50	50	0	0

MY QUANTITATIVE PLAN OF ATTACK

My Raw Score Goal: _____   Questions to Attempt: _____

Questions to Skip: _____   Missable Questions: _____

❏ Note there are 2 Quantitative sections on the SSAT. The number of questions you should skip or you can miss are for both sections together.

Beating the SSAT

❑ Never leave an easy problem blank.

On an easy problem, an answer that instinctively seems right usually is. When the test writers construct a standardized test, they keep in mind the average student. They want the average student to answer the easy problems correctly and the difficult problems incorrectly.

Do not make the early problems harder than they really are. If all else fails, go with your hunch.

❑ Avoid attractors.

The test writers predict potential mistakes by students and include those mistakes as answer choices. In other words, they set traps for the unsuspecting student. We call these answer choices "attractors." Attractors show up most often on medium and difficult problems.

TRY IT OUT

Try to spot the attractor answer choices in the following problems.
Consider how a student might mistakenly choose each attractor answer.

1. $\frac{3}{4} + \frac{1}{3} =$

   (A) $\frac{1}{4}$

   (B) $\frac{4}{7}$

   (C) 1

   (D) $1\frac{1}{12}$

   (E) $1\frac{1}{3}$

Making Your Best Guess

❏ If you can certainly eliminate at least two answers, you should guess from the remaining answer choices. The more answers you can eliminate, the greater advantage you have.

Once you have eliminated an answer, cross it out in the test booklet. This prevents you from wasting time looking at eliminated answers over and over.

Note: Be careful using the guessing strategy on the difficult problems. When you eliminate an answer, be absolutely sure you have a legitimate reason for doing so. Once you've eliminated all the answers you can, guess from the remaining answer choices.

Assume you don't know how to solve the following math problem.
Which answer choices should you eliminate and why?

(Hint: The figure is drawn to scale.)

In the figure above, $x =$

(A) 110
(B) 90
(C) 80
(D) 60
(E) 45

On the following 20 questions, assume you have correctly eliminated answer choices B and D. Try to guess the right answer for each question by filling in an oval for each.

1.   Ⓐ ⊗ Ⓒ ⊗ Ⓔ
2.   Ⓐ ⊗ Ⓒ ⊗ Ⓔ
3.   Ⓐ ⊗ Ⓒ ⊗ Ⓔ
4.   Ⓐ ⊗ Ⓒ ⊗ Ⓔ
5.   Ⓐ ⊗ Ⓒ ⊗ Ⓔ
6.   Ⓐ ⊗ Ⓒ ⊗ Ⓔ
7.   Ⓐ ⊗ Ⓒ ⊗ Ⓔ
8.   Ⓐ ⊗ Ⓒ ⊗ Ⓔ
9.   Ⓐ ⊗ Ⓒ ⊗ Ⓔ
10. Ⓐ ⊗ Ⓒ ⊗ Ⓔ
11. Ⓐ ⊗ Ⓒ ⊗ Ⓔ
12. Ⓐ ⊗ Ⓒ ⊗ Ⓔ
13. Ⓐ ⊗ Ⓒ ⊗ Ⓔ
14. Ⓐ ⊗ Ⓒ ⊗ Ⓔ
15. Ⓐ ⊗ Ⓒ ⊗ Ⓔ
16. Ⓐ ⊗ Ⓒ ⊗ Ⓔ
17. Ⓐ ⊗ Ⓒ ⊗ Ⓔ
18. Ⓐ ⊗ Ⓒ ⊗ Ⓔ
19. Ⓐ ⊗ Ⓒ ⊗ Ⓔ
20. Ⓐ ⊗ Ⓒ ⊗ Ⓔ

RIGHT   _____

$-\frac{1}{4}$ × (# WRONG)   _____

= RAW SCORE   _____

Unless you were extremely unlucky, you probably received a positive raw score (versus zero if you had chosen to leave these questions blank), and, of course, a higher raw score means a higher scaled score and percentile rank.

Answers to above exercise:

1. C   2. A   3. E   4. A   5. A   6. C   7. E   8. C   9. A   10. E

11. A   12. C   13. E   14. E   15. C   16. E   17. A   18. C   19. E   20. A

Using the Answer Choices

❑ On a multiple-choice test, the answer choices can provide you with further ammunition to solve the problem. Don't get stuck trying to find an answer with a certain method. If you can't solve the problem in the forward direction, try to solve in the reverse direction by using the answer choices.

Megan ate $\frac{1}{3}$ of her jellybeans, and then threw five away. If she had 25 jellybeans left, how many did she start with?

(A) 32
(B) 35
(C) 40
(D) 45
(E) 50

Take answer (B) and step through the problem. If Megan had 35 jellybeans and ate $\frac{1}{3}$ of them, she would eat $11\frac{2}{3}$ jellybeans.

It is unlikely that she would eat a fraction of a jellybean, so you should look for an answer choice which is evenly divisible by 3.

Answer (D) 45, might work. If she ate $\frac{1}{3}$ of 45 (15) and then threw 5 away, she would have 25 left. (D) is correct.

TRY IT OUT

Use your answer choices to find the correct answer.

1. If $2x^2 - 3x + 6 = 15$, then x equals

    (A) 2
    (B) 3
    (C) 4
    (D) 6
    (E) 9

General Tactics

❑ Focus on one question at a time.

The SSAT is timed, so it's normal to feel pressure to rush. Resist the temptation to think about the 10 questions ahead of you or the question you did a minute ago. Relax and focus on one question at a time. Believe it or not, **patience** on the SSAT is what allows you to work more quickly and accurately.

❑ Carefully read and think about each question.

Before you jump to the answers, start scribbling things down, or do calculations, make sure you understand exactly what the question is asking.

❑ In SSAT problems (especially math problems), every bit of information is important and useful.

❑ Write in your test booklet.

When you're ready to solve the problem, use the space in your test booklet. Cross out incorrect answers, write down calculations to avoid careless errors, summarize reading passages, etc. Write down whatever will help you solve the problem.

❑ Memorize the format and instructions before you take the test. At test time, you can skip the instructions and focus on the problems.

Chapter Review

❑ General Test-Taking

Your SSAT preparation will focus on learning strategies and strengthening core skills.

Your responsibilities include doing 1-2 hours of homework per session and learning as much vocabulary as you can.

Except for the Reading Comprehension, groups of questions progress from easy to difficult.

❑ Answering Questions

Put your time and energy into the problems you're most capable of answering.

Don't leave easy problems blank. If an answer seems right, it probably is.

Beware of attractors on medium and difficult problems.

Educated guessing will raise your score.

Use the answer choices to help you solve the problems.

SUMMIT
EDUCATIONAL
GROUP

Quantitative

❑ General Information   18

❑ SSAT Structure   19

❑ Plugging In   20

❑ Solving Backwards   22

❑ Choosing Numbers   24

❑ Math Tips   26

General Information

❑ Format/Directions

The quantitative section of the SSAT has two sections with 25 questions each. The questions go from easy to difficult.

❑ Directions are as follows:

Following each problem in this section, there are five suggested answers. Work each problem in your head or in the blank space provided at the right of the page. Then look at the five suggested answers and decide which one is best.

Note: Figures that accompany problems in this section are drawn as accurately as possible EXCEPT when it is stated in a specific problem that its figure is not drawn to scale.

Sample Problem:

$$4,412$$
$$-2,826$$

(A) 1,586
(B) 1,596
(C) 1,696
(D) 2,586
(E) 2,686

SSAT Structure

Writing Sample – 25 minutes

Quantitative – 30 minutes

MATHEMATICS																								
1	2	3	4	5	6	7	8	9	10	11	12	13	14	15	16	17	18	19	20	21	22	23	24	25
EASY					→			MEDIUM				→			DIFFICULT									

Reading Comprehension – 40 minutes

READING PASSAGES																																							
1	2	3	4	5	6	7	8	9	10	11	12	13	14	15	16	17	18	19	20	21	22	23	24	25	26	27	28	29	30	31	32	33	34	35	36	37	38	39	40
NOT IN ORDER OF DIFFICULTY																																							

Verbal – 30 minutes

SYNONYMS																													
1	2	3	4	5	6	7	8	9	10	11	12	13	14	15	16	17	18	19	20	21	22	23	24	25	26	27	28	29	30
EASY					→			MEDIUM				→			DIFFICULT														

ANALOGIES																													
31	32	33	34	35	36	37	38	39	40	41	42	43	44	45	46	47	48	49	50	51	52	53	54	55	56	57	58	59	60
EASY					→			MEDIUM				→			DIFFICULT														

Quantitative – 30 minutes

MATHEMATICS																								
1	2	3	4	5	6	7	8	9	10	11	12	13	14	15	16	17	18	19	20	21	22	23	24	25
EASY					→			MEDIUM				→			DIFFICULT									

Plugging In

❑ Some SSAT math questions can be solved quickly by using the answer choices.

Questions involving algebraic equations can often be solved by plugging in the answer choices for a variable.

> If $7x - 3 = 46$, then $x =$
>
> (A) 0
> (B) 1
> (C) 5
> (D) 7
> (E) 9
>
> If you start with (C), you get $7(5) - 3 = 46$, or $32 = 46$ (not a true statement). So, x must be bigger than 5, because 32 is too small.
>
> Eliminate (A) and (B), because these will make your quantity smaller.
>
> Try (D) and (E).
>
> The correct answer is (D) because $7(7) - 3 = 46$.

❑ When plugging in, start with answer choice (C).

Since numerical answer choices are presented in either ascending or descending order, choice (C) will be in the middle. If (C) isn't right, you might be able to tell if you need a larger or smaller number. By starting in the middle, you can reduce the number of answer choices you plug in, which will save you time.

PUT IT TOGETHER

Solve the following equations by plugging in:

1. If $2 \times (N + 5) = 100$, then $N =$

   (A) 10
   (B) 25
   (C) 40
   (D) 45
   (E) 50

---

2. If $\dfrac{500}{25} + \dfrac{70}{25} + \dfrac{A}{25} = 23$, what is A?

   (A) 0
   (B) 2
   (C) 5
   (D) 15
   (E) 25

---

3. Which value of N does NOT satisfy $\dfrac{N}{4} + \dfrac{2}{3} > \dfrac{1}{6}$?

   (A) 2
   (B) 1
   (C) 0
   (D) −1
   (E) −2

---

4. John is x years old and Paul is 8 years older than John. If in 4 years Paul will be twice as old as John, then how old is John now?

   (A) 4
   (B) 8
   (C) 12
   (D) 16
   (E) 20

Solving Backwards

❑ Many word problems can be solved by using the answer choices to work backward. This may be easier than trying to set up an algebraic equation.

> Out of 73 black and white socks in a drawer, there are 23 more white socks than there are black socks. How many white socks are there?
>
> (A) 23
> (B) 25
> (C) 45
> (D) 48
> (E) 50
>
>
>
> Now go to the answer choices.
>
> Start with (C).
> If there are 45 white socks, there are 22 black socks (45 – 23 = 22). This gives a total of 67 socks. Since 67 is less than 73, we know there must be more than 45 white socks. So your choices are (D) or (E).
>
> Let's try (E).
> If there are 50 white socks, there are 27 black socks (50 – 23 = 27). This gives 77 total socks. Incorrect.
>
> The answer must be (D), but let's check it.
> 48 white socks means there are 25 black socks (48 – 23 = 25).
> 48 + 25 = 73. (D) is correct.

❑ Use the answer choices as a guide for how to solve questions.

❑ Some questions are so complicated that it is hard to put all of the information together. It often helps to look at what the question is asking you for and then to consider what you need to do to find that information.

PUT IT TOGETHER

Use the answer choices to solve the following word problems:

1. There are 5 times as many pairs of white socks as there are
    pairs of black socks in Jason's drawer. If the total number of
    pairs of socks equals 36, then how many pairs of white socks
    are in the drawer?

    (A) 3
    (B) 6
    (C) 15
    (D) 18
    (E) 30

2. George and Bessie both collect stamps. If George has 22
    stamps and Bessie 38 stamps, how many stamps must George
    purchase from Bessie if they are to have the same number of
    stamps in their collections?

    (A) 4
    (B) 8
    (C) 16
    (D) 18
    (E) 26

3. 24 feet of fence enclose Dan's rectangular yard. What's the
    yard's width, if the width is $\frac{1}{3}$ of the length?

    (A) 3 feet
    (B) 6 feet
    (C) 9 feet
    (D) 18 feet
    (E) 64 feet

Choosing Numbers

❑ Some questions may seem difficult because they feel too abstract. You can make some questions more concrete and easier to solve by giving values to variables.

❑ When a question has expressions for answer choices, try choosing numbers for the variables. Make up values and test them out to see which answer choice works.

> Nate bought a burger for B dollars and a soda for S dollars. He paid with a $5 bill. What was the amount of change, in dollars, that Nate received?
>
> (A) $B + S + 5$
> (B) $B - S + 5$
> (C) $B - (S + 5)$
> (D) $5 - (B + S)$
> (E) $5 - (B - S)$

> First, choose values for B and for S.
> Let's make B = $3 and S = $1.
>
> According to the question, if the burger costs $3 and the soda costs $1, Nate should receive $1 in change.
>
> Let's check the answer choices. We'll plug in the values we chose for B and S and see which results in $1 in change:
>
> (A) $3 + $1 + $5 = $9
> (B) $3 − $1 + $5 = $7
> (C) $3 − ($1 + $5) = -$3
> ✓ (D) $5 − ($3 + $1) = $1
> (E) $5 − ($3 − $1) = $3
>
> The correct answer is (D), because when we plug in the numbers we chose, we get the right result.

❑ Depending on the question and the numbers you choose, you might have more than one answer work. If this happens, try different numbers and test those answers again.

PUT IT TOGETHER

1. If *n* is greater than 1, which of the following is greatest?

    (A) $2n+1$
    (B) $n+2$
    (C) $n+1$
    (D) n

    (E) $\dfrac{n}{n}+2$

    _____

2. The price of gasoline was *C* cents at the beginning of the month. What was the price, in cents, after it went down 3 cents, doubled, and then went up 7 cents?

    (A) $C-10$
    (B) $C-4$
    (C) $C+8$
    (D) $2C+1$
    (E) $2C+4$

    _____

3. Olivia paid for a tool with a $100 bill. She received *D* dollars in change. Which of the following expressions tells how many dollars she paid for the tool?

    (A) $\dfrac{100D}{2}$

    (B) $\dfrac{D}{100}$

    (C) $\dfrac{100}{D}$

    (D) $100-D$

    (E) $D-100$

Math Tips

❑ Pay attention to units. Information in a question might be in one unit (such as feet or seconds) while the answer is in another unit (such as yards or minutes).

Know how to convert the following units:

12 inches = 1 foot

3 feet = 1 yard

100 centimeters = 1 meter

1,000 meters = 1 kilometer

60 seconds = 1 minute

60 minutes = 1 hour

❑ If the first answer choice you check is correct, check another answer choice. If more than one answer choice seems right, you may have misunderstood the question or there may be the option to choose "all of the above."

❑ The answer choice "It cannot be determined from the information given" is **rarely** the correct answer. If a question seems impossible, it is best to reread the question and try to solve it in a different way.

Chapter Review

❑ Format/Directions

Questions get harder as you go. The last question in a Quantitative section is much more difficult and takes much longer to solve than the first question, but they are both worth just one point. Pace yourself; work patiently and carefully.

❑ Plugging In

Use answer choices to help you solve problems.

When plugging in, start with answer choice (C).

❑ Solving Backwards

Consider what information the question asks for and think of what you must do to find that information.

Answer choices can sometimes be clues for what type of answer you should get.

❑ Choosing Numbers

In complex equations or word problems, choose values for variables or unknown numbers. This can make abstract problems easier to handle.

SUMMIT
EDUCATIONAL
G R O U P

Number Concepts & Operations

❏ Addition, Subtraction, Multiplication, & Division   32

❏ Odd & Even Integers   36

❏ Positive & Negative Numbers   38

❏ Divisibility & Remainders   40

❏ Multiples & Factors   42

❏ Fractions   46

❏ Place Value   64

❏ Rounding & Estimation   66

❏ Decimals   70

❏ Percents   76

❏ Ratios   82

❏ Proportions   86

❏ Order of Operations   90

❏ Sequences, Patterns, & Logic   92

Number Concepts & Operations

❑   Over half of SSAT math is arithmetic. Mastering arithmetic skills will help you solve
arithmetic problems as well as algebra and geometry problems.

❑   In this chapter, you will:

• learn arithmetic vocabulary including integers, multiples, and divisibility.

• review basic arithmetic concepts like adding, subtracting, multiplying, and dividing.

• review the rules regarding fractions, decimals, and percents.

• learn how to apply these concepts to the types of multiple choice questions that appear
on the SSAT.

Vocabulary

❑ An **integer** is any positive or negative whole number or zero.

{...–3, –2, –1, 0, 1, 2, 3,...}

❑ A **digit** is any whole number from 0 to 9.

{0, 1, 2, 3, 4, 5, 6, 7, 8, 9} is the set of all digits.

❑ A **prime number** is an integer greater than 1 that is divisible only by 1 and itself.

2 is the smallest prime number. It is also the only prime number that is even.

2,3,5,7,11, and 13 are examples of prime numbers.

❑ A **sum** is the result of an addition.

❑ A **difference** is the result of a subtraction.

❑ A **product** is the result of a multiplication.

❑ A **quotient** is the result of a division.

A **dividend** is the number being divided in a division.

A **divisor** is the number dividing in a division.

$$\text{divisor}\overline{)\text{dividend}}^{\text{quotient}}$$

❑ A **base** is a number being raised to an exponent.

An **exponent** is the number of times you multiply a base by itself.

❑ **Consecutive numbers** are whole numbers that increase or decrease incrementally by 1.

{31, 32, 33, 34} and {–2, –1, 0, 1, 2, 3, 4, 5} are sets of consecutive numbers.

Addition, Subtraction, Multiplication, & Division

❑ On SSAT math problems, you will have to calculate sums, differences, products, and quotients. Occasionally, you will have to deal with large numbers.

Work carefully and methodically. If you rush, you are likely to make careless mistakes.

❑ Make sure your answer makes sense. Use logic to check your work.

For instance, if you are multiplying two positive whole numbers and you get an answer that is smaller than the original numbers, you might have made a mistake.

❑ Memorize the following rules.

0 times any number equals 0.
0 divided by any number equals 0.

$91 \times 0 =$ _____ $0 \div 10 =$ _____

1 times a number equals the number.
Any number divided by 1 equals the number.

$2,345 \times 1 =$ _____ $999 \div 1 =$ _____

Any number divided by itself equals 1.

$1,023 \div 1,023 =$ _____

To multiply any number by a power of 10 (10, 100, 1000, etc.), move the decimal place to the right by the number of zeros.

$93 \times 100 =$ _____ $6.34 \times 10,000 =$ _____

To divide any number by a power of 10, move the decimal place to the left by the number of zeros.

$26 \div 10 =$ _____ $2,435 \div 100 =$ _____

TRY IT OUT

1. $11,324 + 89,376 =$

2. $1,001 + 9,999 =$

3. $50 + 1,000 + 100 + 0 =$

4. $6,003 + 9 + 8 =$

5. $10 + 100 + 1,000 + 10,000 =$

6. $6,923 - 3,110 =$

7. $10,294 - 10,294 =$

8. $1,100 - 100 =$

9. $20,000 - 7,000 =$

10. $115 - 30 =$

11. $7 \times 3 =$

12. $27 \times 23 =$

13. $289 \times 100 \times 1 =$

14. $5 \times 4 \times 3 \times 2 \times 1 \times 0 =$

15. $9,999 \times \dfrac{1}{10} =$

16. $286 \div 13 =$

17. $412 \div 1 =$

18. $0 \div 989 =$

19. $34,776 \div 100 =$

20. $\dfrac{99}{99} =$

PUT IT TOGETHER

1. Jeremy has 5 marbles and Evan has 19. How many marbles must Evan give to Jeremy if they are to have the same number?

    (A) 4
    (B) 7
    (C) 9
    (D) 14
    (E) 28

2. If $9 + 9 + 9 + 9 + 9 + 9 + 9 = 7 \times \square$, what is the value of $\square$?

    (A) 7
    (B) 9
    (C) 16
    (D) 56
    (E) 63

3. If $46 + 78 = (10 \times 2) + (1 \times \square) + (100 \times 1)$, then $\square =$

    (A) 2
    (B) 4
    (C) 14
    (D) 24
    (E) 124

4. $8\overline{)648} =$

    (A) $\dfrac{600}{8} \times \dfrac{40}{8} \times \dfrac{8}{8}$

    (B) $\dfrac{6}{8} \times \dfrac{4}{8} \times \dfrac{8}{8}$

    (C) $\dfrac{600}{8} + \dfrac{40}{8} + \dfrac{8}{8}$

    (D) $\dfrac{64}{8} + \dfrac{8}{8}$

    (E) $\dfrac{6}{8} + \dfrac{4}{8} + \dfrac{8}{8}$

$$\begin{array}{r} 4 \\ 89\overline{)37\Box} \\ 35\Box \\ \hline 20 \end{array}$$

5. In the division problem shown above, what digit is
    represented by □ ?

    (A) 0
    (B) 4
    (C) 6
    (D) 8
    (E) 9

---

        8   6   7   5   3

6. The five digits shown above can form a three-digit
    number and a two-digit number by using each digit once.
    Of the pairs of numbers that can be formed, which three-
    digit number divided by the two-digit number will have
    the smallest quotient?

    (A) $358 \div 67$
    (B) $358 \div 76$
    (C) $653 \div 78$
    (D) $876 \div 35$
    (E) $876 \div 53$

---

7. For which of the following would the result be greater if
    the number 50 is used instead of 60?

    I. $60 - 100$

    II. $100 - 60$

    III. $\dfrac{100}{60}$

    (A) I only
    (B) II only
    (C) III only
    (D) II and III only
    (E) I, II, and III

Odd & Even Integers

❑ An **odd number** is an integer that is not divisible by 2.

{...−5, −3, −1, 1, 3, 5,...}

❑ An **even number** is an integer that is divisible by 2.

{...−6, −4, −2, 0, 2, 4, 6,...}

❑ Even and odd integers follow certain rules when added, subtracted, or multiplied.

It can be helpful to memorize these rules. You may also test a few numbers to remember the rules when you need to.

even ± even = even

0 + 4 = 4	8 − even number = _____

even ± odd = odd

4 + 3 = 7	9 − even number = _____

odd ± odd = even

7 − 5 = 2	3 + odd number = _____

even × even = even

6 × 6 = 36	2 × even number = _____

even × odd = even

4 × 3 = 12	2 × odd number = _____

odd × odd = odd

7 × 11 = 77	3 × odd number = _____

TRY IT OUT

1. Which of the following could be the result of adding two even integers?

    {1, 3, 4, 6, 11, 17, 23, 99, 400}

2. Which of the following could be the result of subtracting two odd integers?

    {−3, 0, 1, 5, 12, 18, 100, 101}

3. Which of the following could be the result of multiplying two odd integers?

    {0, 1, 3, 4, 8, 11, 21, 24, 90}

PUT IT TOGETHER

1. If x and y are both odd integers, which of the following is NOT an odd integer?

    (A) xy
    (B) $3xy$
    (C) $x - y$
    (D) $2x - y$
    (E) $2x + y$

2. $18 \times K$

    For which of the following values of K will the product above be an odd number?

    (A) 9
    (B) 2
    (C) 1
    (D) 0
    (E) 0.5

3. If x is an even integer, which of the following must also be even?

    I. $x + 1$
    II. $x + 2$
    III. $2x$
    IV. $3x$

    (A) II and III only
    (B) II and IV only
    (C) III and IV only
    (D) II, III, and IV only
    (E) I, II, III, and IV

Positive & Negative Numbers

❑ A **positive number** is any number that is greater than 0.

$$\{1, 3, 2.4, \frac{6}{7}\}$$

❑ A **negative number** is any number that is less than 0.

$$\{-3.5, -57, -\frac{1}{2}, -.273\}$$

❑ Negative numbers follow certain rules when being added, subtracted, multiplied, or divided.

Adding a negative number is the same as subtracting a positive number.

$$4 + (-3) = 4 - 3 \qquad\qquad 0 + (-5) = \underline{\hspace{2cm}}$$

Subtracting a negative number is the same as adding a positive number.

$$4 - (-3) = 4 + 3 \qquad\qquad 0 - (-5) = \underline{\hspace{2cm}}$$

A negative number multiplied or divided by a negative number gives a positive number.

$$(-10) \times (-2) = 20 \qquad\qquad (-12) \div (-4) = \underline{\hspace{2cm}}$$

A negative number multiplied by a positive number (or vice versa) gives a negative number.

A negative number divided by a positive number (or vice versa) gives a negative number.

$$(-10) \times (2) = -20 \qquad\qquad (12) \times (-4) = \underline{\hspace{2cm}}$$

TRY IT OUT

1. $-5 + 2 =$

2. $-3 + 4 =$

3. $-1 + 8 =$

4. $-9 + 9 =$

5. $6 + (-5) =$

6. $1 + (-2) =$

7. $-5 - 7 =$

8. $-1 - 4 =$

9. $14 - (-9) =$

10. $-8 - (-4) =$

11. $-1 - (-9) =$

12. $3 \times (-5) =$

13. $-20 \div 2 =$

14. $(-2) \times (-6) =$

15. $(-60) \div (-15) =$

PUT IT TOGETHER

1. If the positive number N is multiplied by a number less than 0, the product <u>must</u> be

    (A) less than N
    (B) 0
    (C) greater than 0
    (D) greater than N
    (E) It cannot be determined from the information given.

    ---

2. If x and y are negative integers, which of the following must be a negative number?

    (A) xy

    (B) $\dfrac{x}{y}$

    (C) $\dfrac{y}{x}$

    (D) $x - y$
    (E) $x + y$

Divisibility & Remainders

❑ A number is **divisible** by another number if it can be evenly divided by that number with no remainder.

> 25 is divisible by 5 because 25 ÷ 5 = 5 with no remainder.
>
> 25 is not divisible by 6 because 25 ÷ 6 = 4 with a remainder of 1.

❑ When a number does not divide evenly into another number, the number that remains at the end of the division is called the **remainder**. The remainder is always less than the divisor.

> 23 ÷ 5 equals 4 with a remainder of 3.
>
> $$\begin{array}{r} 4\ R3 \\ 5\overline{)23} \\ 20 \\ \hline 3 \end{array}$$

You can check your answer by multiplying the divisor by the quotient and adding the remainder. This should equal the original dividend.

(divisor × quotient) + remainder = dividend

> 23 ÷ 5 equals 4 with a remainder of 3.
>
> (5 × 4) + 3 = 23

TRY IT OUT

1. Is 8 divisible by 2?

2. Is 36 divisible by 8?

3. What is the remainder when 30 is divided by 7?

4. What is the remainder when 30 is divided by 6?

5. What is the remainder when 7 is divided by 30?

PUT IT TOGETHER

1. Heather wants to buy shirts for her 15 employees. There are 4 shirts in each package. How many packages of shirts must she buy in order for each employee to have a shirt?

   (A) 3
   (B) 4
   (C) 5
   (D) 11
   (E) 60

2. When x is divided by 6, the remainder is 5. Which of the following could have remainder 1 when divided by 6?

   (A) $x - 3$
   (B) $x - 2$
   (C) $x - 1$
   (D) $x + 1$
   (E) $x + 2$

$$741\overline{)2,96\square} \quad 4\,R3$$

3. In the division problem above, what digit is represented by $\square$?

   (A) 1
   (B) 3
   (C) 4
   (D) 7
   (E) 9

Multiples & Factors

❑ A **multiple** is the product of a particular number and another number.

> 4, 8, 12, and 20 are all multiples of 4:
>
> $4 = 4 \times 1$ $8 = 4 \times 2$ $12 = 4 \times 3$ $20 = 4 \times 5$

❑ A **factor** of a number is a number that divides evenly into that number.

> 6 is a factor of 24 because 6 divides evenly into 24.
>
> 6 and 4 are called a pair of factors, because 6 × 4 = 24.

❑ To find the **prime factorization** of a number, factor the number until all factors are prime. The prime factorization of a number is the product of its prime factors.

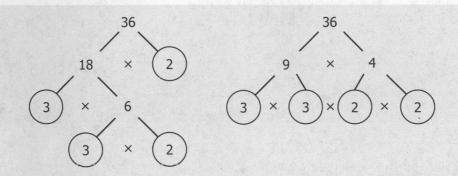

> The prime factorization of 36 is 3 × 3 × 2 × 2.
>
> Note: no matter which two factors you start with, you'll get the same result.

TRY IT OUT

1. List all the pairs of factors of 32.

2. List all of the pairs of factors of 63.

3. List 5 multiples of 2.

4. List 3 multiples of 12.

5. Find the prime factorizations of 24, 84, and 100.

PUT IT TOGETHER

1. In a group of eight friends, each friend is given the same number of tickets, with no tickets left over. Which of the following could be the total number of tickets given out?

    (A) 12
    (B) 30
    (C) 52
    (D) 60
    (E) 96

2. A crate holds 2 dozen bottles in each layer, and there are three layers in each crate. If a warehouse contains only full crates of bottles, which of the following could be the number of bottles in the warehouse?

    (A) 120
    (B) 140
    (C) 146
    (D) 206
    (E) 216

3. If $\frac{x}{4}$ is a whole number, then x could be

    (A) 1
    (B) 6
    (C) 10
    (D) 12
    (E) 13

Checkpoint Review

1. Which number could be the sum of three consecutive positive odd integers?

   (A) 114
   (B) 115
   (C) 116
   (D) 117
   (E) 118

2. In a physical education class, all of the students are grouped into teams. Each student can only be in one team. If there are 40 students in the class and up to 6 students can be in each team, what is the smallest number of teams into which the class can be grouped?

   (A) 7
   (B) 6
   (C) 5
   (D) 4
   (E) 3

3. Jhumpa is saving money for a $400 guitar. If she begins with $80 and saves an additional $45 each month, how many months will she have to save money until she can afford the guitar?

   (A) 6
   (B) 7
   (C) 8
   (D) 9
   (E) 10

4. A car rental costs $60 per day and an additional $0.15 for each mile traveled. If a customer rents a car for 3 days and travels 180 miles, what would be total price for the rental?

   (A) $87.00
   (B) $182.70
   (C) $207.00
   (D) $330.00
   (E) $450.00

Checkpoint Review

5. In the middle of a game, Team A was winning by 7 points. In the end, Team B won by 4 points. If Team A scored 13 points in the second half of the game, how many points did Team B score in the second half of the game?

    (A) 2
    (B) 10
    (C) 11
    (D) 21
    (E) 24

6. A group of 16 people are waiting for boats to carry them across a river. A maximum of 6 people can be in each boat. If no two boats can carry the same number of people, what is the smallest number of boats needed to carry all 16 people?

    (A) 2
    (B) 3
    (C) 4
    (D) 5
    (E) 6

7. If x and y are distinct integers, and the value of $(y \div x)$ is an even integer, then which statement is true?

    (A) the product of x and y must be even
    (B) the product of x and y must be odd
    (C) x must be even
    (D) x must be odd
    (E) $(x \div y)$ must result in an even integer

8. $m + n$ represents a non-zero number divisible by 11. Which of the following must also be divisible by 11?

    (A) $m \times n$
    (B) $m - n$
    (C) $m + 10n$
    (D) $10m + n$
    (E) $10m + 10n$

Fractions

❑ Fractions are used to represent portions of a whole. Fractions are written as $\dfrac{\text{PART}}{\text{WHOLE}}$.

Fractions also represent divisions, with the part divided by the whole.

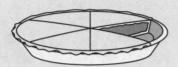

The pie above is divided into 6 equal parts.

One part, or $\dfrac{1}{6}$ of the pie, is missing. Five parts, or $\dfrac{5}{6}$ of the pie, are left.

❑ The **numerator** is the top part of a fraction. The **denominator** is the bottom part.

❑ An **improper fraction** has a numerator that is greater than or equal to the denominator.

❑ A **mixed number** is made up of a whole number and a fraction. It is equal to the sum of the whole number and the fraction.

$$1\frac{3}{8}=1+\frac{3}{8} \qquad\qquad\qquad\qquad 2\frac{5}{6}=\underline{\hspace{2cm}}$$

❑ To convert a mixed number to an improper fraction, rewrite the whole number as a fraction with the same denominator. Then, add the two fractions.

Convert $2\dfrac{3}{5}$ to an improper fraction:

$$2\frac{3}{5} \implies \frac{10}{5}+\frac{3}{5} \implies \frac{13}{5} \qquad\qquad 4\frac{3}{4}=\underline{\hspace{2cm}}$$

❑ To convert an improper fraction to a mixed number, divide the numerator by the denominator. The whole number of the dividend will be the whole number and the remainder will be the numerator of the fraction.

$$\frac{17}{5} \implies 5\overline{)17}^{\,3\text{ R}2} \implies 3\frac{2}{5} \qquad\qquad \frac{40}{6}=\underline{\hspace{2cm}}$$

TRY IT OUT

Convert mixed numbers to improper fractions:

1. $1\dfrac{1}{4}$

2. $6\dfrac{2}{3}$

3. $5\dfrac{6}{7}$

Convert improper fractions to mixed numbers:

4. $\dfrac{3}{2}$

5. $\dfrac{8}{3}$

6. $\dfrac{19}{4}$

Solve:

7. If half a number is 5, what is the whole number?

8. If one third of a number is 4, what is the whole number?

9. If $\dfrac{4}{9}$ of a number is 7, what is $\dfrac{8}{9}$ of the number?

10. If $\dfrac{3}{4}$ of a number is 15, what is $\dfrac{1}{4}$ of the number?

11. If $\dfrac{4}{7}$ of a number is 40, what is the whole number?

12. If there are 300 calories in a $\dfrac{2}{3}$-cup serving of granola, how many calories are there in a 1-cup serving?

PUT IT TOGETHER

1. $\left(4\times\dfrac{1}{4}\right)+\left(3\times\dfrac{1}{3}\right)=$

   (A) 0

   (B) $\dfrac{4}{7}$

   (C) 1

   (D) $\dfrac{7}{4}$

   (E) 2

---

2. When a cake is cut into 8 even slices instead of 12 even slices, which of the following must be true?

   (A) each slice will be smaller
   (B) some slices will have different sizes
   (C) there will be 4 more slices
   (D) each slice will be larger
   (E) 2 of the slices will be twice as large

---

3. When 30 gallons of water were poured into an empty tank, the water filled $\dfrac{2}{3}$ of the tank's total capacity. What is the tank's total capacity in gallons?

   (A) 20
   (B) 40
   (C) 45
   (D) 60
   (E) 75

---

4. If n is greater than 1, then $\dfrac{1}{n}$ must be

   (A) less than 0
   (B) less than 1
   (C) greater than 1
   (D) greater than n
   (E) between 1 and n

5. If x and y are not equal to zero, what is the value of
    $\dfrac{6x}{6x} - \dfrac{3y}{3y}$?

    (A) -1
    (B) 0
    (C) 1
    (D) 2
    (E) It cannot be determined from the information given.

6. If $\dfrac{m}{n} = 1$, and m and n are non-zero integers, which of the
    following must be true?

    (A) m is greater than n
    (B) n is greater than m
    (C) $m = y - 1$
    (D) $m = 1$
    (E) $m = n$

7. If $\dfrac{2}{3}$ of a number is 18, then $\dfrac{4}{3}$ of the number is

    (A) 6
    (B) 9
    (C) 27
    (D) 36
    (E) 72

8. A jug that is $\dfrac{3}{5}$ full contains 15 ounces of liquid. How
    many ounces of liquid does the jug hold when it's full?

    (A) 9
    (B) 10
    (C) 24
    (D) 25
    (E) 45

Reducing Fractions

❑ In general, fractions should be written in their reduced forms. To reduce fractions, divide the top and bottom by a common factor. Continue to divide by common factors until the top and bottom have no more common factors.

> Reduce $\dfrac{12}{30}$.
>
> 2 is a common factor of 12 and 30. Divide both 12 and 30 by 2.
>
> $$\dfrac{12 \div 2}{30 \div 2} = \dfrac{6}{15}$$
>
> 3 is a common factor of 6 and 15. Divide both 6 and 15 by 3.
>
> $$\dfrac{6 \div 3}{15 \div 3} = \dfrac{2}{5}$$
>
> There is no factor that divides into 2 and 5, so $\dfrac{2}{5}$ is reduced completely.

❑ The **lowest common denominator** of a group of fractions is the smallest number that each of the denominators will divide into. Finding a common denominator is the first step in adding or subtracting fractions. Finding a common denominator also lets you compare the relative sizes of fractions.

> What is the LCD of $\dfrac{3}{4}$, $\dfrac{1}{2}$, $\dfrac{2}{3}$? Arrange the fractions from smallest to largest.
>
> The LCD is 12. 12 is the smallest number that 2, 3, and 4 will divide into.
>
> Rewriting the fractions with the LCD, we get:
>
> $$\dfrac{3 \times 3}{4 \times 3} = \dfrac{9}{12} \qquad \dfrac{1 \times 6}{2 \times 6} = \dfrac{6}{12} \qquad \dfrac{2 \times 4}{3 \times 4} = \dfrac{8}{12}$$
>
> Fractions arranged from smallest to largest:
>
> $$\dfrac{1}{2} = \dfrac{6}{12}, \quad \dfrac{2}{3} = \dfrac{8}{12}, \quad \dfrac{3}{4} = \dfrac{9}{12}$$

TRY IT OUT

Reduce the following fractions:

1. $\dfrac{14}{21}$

2. $\dfrac{26}{30}$

3. $\dfrac{45}{100}$

4. $\dfrac{28}{63}$

Find the lowest common denominator for each group of fractions, and arrange the fractions from smallest to largest:

5. $\dfrac{3}{8}, \dfrac{4}{3}, \dfrac{1}{3}$

6. $\dfrac{2}{5}, \dfrac{3}{8}, \dfrac{3}{4}$

7. $\dfrac{7}{30}, \dfrac{1}{6}, \dfrac{4}{5}, \dfrac{8}{15}$

8. $\dfrac{1}{2}, \dfrac{2}{3}, \dfrac{3}{7}, \dfrac{4}{5}$

PUT IT TOGETHER

1. Which of the following is greater than $\frac{2}{3}$?

   (A) $\frac{1}{2}$

   (B) $\frac{3}{4}$

   (C) $\frac{3}{5}$

   (D) $\frac{4}{7}$

   (E) $\frac{5}{8}$

2. All of the following are true EXCEPT

   (A) $\frac{1}{2} < \frac{3}{5}$

   (B) $\frac{1}{3} < \frac{2}{5}$

   (C) $\frac{3}{4} < \frac{3}{5}$

   (D) $\frac{7}{8} < \frac{8}{9}$

   (E) $\frac{4}{7} < \frac{5}{8}$

3. If $\frac{1}{2}$ of a number is 200, then $\frac{2}{5}$ of the number is

   (A) less than 200
   (B) greater than 200
   (C) greater than the number
   (D) equal to 200
   (E) equal to the number

4. $2\frac{2}{3}$ is equal to how many sixths?

   (A) 4
   (B) 8
   (C) 10
   (D) 14
   (E) 16

Adding & Subtracting Fractions

❑ To add fractions, first adjust the fractions so they have a common denominator. Then add the numerators only and keep the common denominator.

$$\frac{1}{3} + \frac{1}{2} =$$

lowest common denominator = 6.

$$\frac{1 \times 2}{3 \times 2} = \frac{2}{6} \text{ and } \frac{1 \times 3}{2 \times 3} = \frac{3}{6}$$

So, $\frac{1}{3} + \frac{1}{2}$ ⇨ $\frac{2}{6} + \frac{3}{6}$ ⇨ $\frac{2+3}{6}$ ⇨ $\frac{5}{6}$

❑ To subtract fractions, first adjust the fractions so they have a common denominator. Then subtract the numerators only.

$$\frac{3}{4} - \frac{1}{3} \Rightarrow \frac{9}{12} - \frac{4}{12} \Rightarrow \frac{5}{12}$$

When subtracting fractions, it often helps to convert mixed numbers to improper fractions before subtracting.

TRY IT OUT

1. $\dfrac{1}{3} + \dfrac{1}{3}$

2. $\dfrac{1}{2} + \dfrac{1}{3}$

3. $\dfrac{1}{2} + \dfrac{1}{6}$

4. $\dfrac{1}{12} + \dfrac{2}{3}$

5. $\dfrac{3}{10} + \dfrac{5}{6}$

6. $\dfrac{1}{3} + \dfrac{1}{6} + \dfrac{4}{9}$

7. $1\dfrac{1}{3} + \dfrac{1}{6}$

8. $5\dfrac{1}{3} + 2\dfrac{1}{2}$

9. $\dfrac{2}{3} - \dfrac{1}{3}$

10. $\dfrac{1}{2} - \dfrac{1}{4}$

11. $\dfrac{2}{5} - \dfrac{1}{10}$

12. $\dfrac{5}{12} - \dfrac{1}{3}$

13. $\dfrac{6}{7} - \dfrac{1}{2}$

14. $7 - \dfrac{1}{3}$

15. $2\dfrac{1}{2} \quad 1\dfrac{1}{2}$

16. $3\dfrac{1}{3} - 1\dfrac{5}{6}$

17. $4\dfrac{3}{5} - 2\dfrac{1}{5}$

PUT IT TOGETHER

1. $300 - 2\frac{8}{9} =$

    (A) $299\frac{1}{9}$

    (B) $298\frac{8}{9}$

    (C) $298\frac{1}{9}$

    (D) $297\frac{8}{9}$

    (E) $297\frac{1}{9}$

    _____

2. $3\frac{1}{6} + 1\frac{5}{6} + 5\frac{5}{6} =$

    (A) $9\frac{5}{6}$

    (B) 10

    (C) $10\frac{1}{6}$

    (D) $10\frac{5}{6}$

    (E) $11\frac{1}{6}$

    _____

3. $17\left(\frac{6}{51} - \frac{2}{17}\right) =$

    (A) 16
    (B) 4
    (C) 2
    (D) 1
    (E) 0

4. If $\dfrac{1}{3}+\dfrac{x}{12}=1$, then $x=$

    (A) 8
    (B) 6
    (C) 4
    (D) 3
    (E) 2

    _____

5. If $\dfrac{4}{16}+\dfrac{1}{4}=\dfrac{x}{20}$, then $x=$

    (A) 5
    (B) 10
    (C) 15
    (D) 20
    (E) 40

    _____

6. Adding which of the following to $\dfrac{3}{7}$ will give a sum that

    is greater than 1?

    (A) $\dfrac{3}{7}$

    (B) $\dfrac{4}{7}$

    (C) $\dfrac{1}{2}$

    (D) $\dfrac{2}{5}$

    (E) $\dfrac{5}{8}$

Multiplying & Dividing Fractions

❑ To multiply fractions, multiply straight across.

First, convert mixed numbers to improper fractions.

If possible, cross-simplify before multiplying. To cross-simplify, look for common factors between the numerator of your first fraction and the denominator of your second fraction, or between the denominator of your first fraction and the numerator of your second fraction.

$$1\frac{4}{5}\times\frac{1}{6} \quad\Rightarrow\quad \frac{9}{5}\times\frac{1}{6} \quad\Rightarrow\quad \frac{\overset{3}{\cancel{9}}}{5}\times\frac{1}{\underset{2}{\cancel{6}}} \quad\Rightarrow\quad \frac{3}{5}\times\frac{1}{2} \quad\Rightarrow\quad \frac{3\times1}{5\times2} \quad\Rightarrow\quad \frac{3}{10}$$

Remember, you should only cross-simplify when fractions are being <u>multiplied</u>.

❑ Two numbers are **reciprocals** if their product is 1.

The reciprocal of 4 is $\frac{1}{4}$ because $4\times\frac{1}{4}=1$.

To find the reciprocal of a fraction, "flip" the fraction by switching its numerator and denominator.

The reciprocal of $\frac{2}{5}$ is $\frac{5}{2}$.

❑ To divide fractions, multiply by the reciprocal of the divisor.

$$\frac{1}{3}\div\frac{1}{2} \quad\Rightarrow\quad \frac{1}{3}\div\frac{1}{2} \quad\Rightarrow\quad \frac{1}{3}\times\frac{2}{1} \quad\Rightarrow\quad \frac{2}{3}$$

TRY IT OUT

1. $\dfrac{2}{3} \times \dfrac{1}{7}$

2. $\dfrac{1}{3} \times \dfrac{3}{5}$

3. $\dfrac{4}{5} \times \dfrac{1}{2}$

4. $\dfrac{3}{4} \times \dfrac{8}{15}$

5. $\dfrac{3}{7} \times \dfrac{14}{15}$

6. $\dfrac{3}{4} \times 16$

7. $5 \times \dfrac{5}{6}$

8. $\dfrac{7}{8} \times 24$

9. $\dfrac{1}{2} \div \dfrac{1}{3}$

10. $\dfrac{2}{5} \div \dfrac{1}{5}$

11. $\dfrac{2}{3} \div \dfrac{5}{6}$

12. $\dfrac{3}{7} \div \dfrac{9}{14}$

13. $4\dfrac{1}{3} \div \dfrac{5}{6}$

14. $2\dfrac{2}{7} \div \dfrac{4}{7}$

15. $12 \div \dfrac{2}{5}$

16. $14 \div \dfrac{2}{7}$

PUT IT TOGETHER

1. All of the following are equal EXCEPT

    (A) $1 \times \dfrac{2}{4}$

    (B) $\dfrac{4}{1} \times \dfrac{3}{6}$

    (C) $3 \times \dfrac{1}{6}$

    (D) $\dfrac{15}{6} \times \dfrac{1}{5}$

    (E) $\dfrac{2}{3} \times \dfrac{3}{4}$

2. 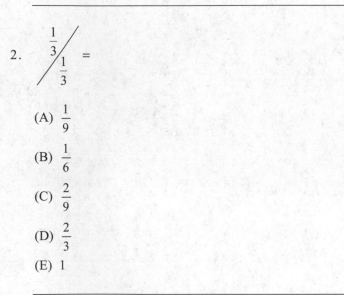 $\dfrac{\frac{1}{3}}{\frac{1}{3}} =$

    (A) $\dfrac{1}{9}$

    (B) $\dfrac{1}{6}$

    (C) $\dfrac{2}{9}$

    (D) $\dfrac{2}{3}$

    (E) 1

3. Which of the following products is greatest?

    (A) $\dfrac{1}{3} \times \dfrac{1}{6}$

    (B) $\dfrac{1}{4} \times \dfrac{1}{5}$

    (C) $\dfrac{1}{7} \times \dfrac{1}{4}$

    (D) $\dfrac{1}{8} \times \dfrac{1}{2}$

    (E) $\dfrac{1}{5} \times \dfrac{1}{5}$

4. A piece of fabric that is $4\frac{1}{2}$ feet long can be cut into how many pieces that are each 3 inches long?

   (A) 12
   (B) 13
   (C) 14
   (D) 17
   (E) 18

---

5. Which of the following is a way to compute the product $2\frac{1}{3}\times15$?

   (A) $(2\times15)+\left(\dfrac{1}{3}\times15\right)$

   (B) $\left(\dfrac{1}{3}\times2\right)+\left(\dfrac{1}{3}\times15\right)$

   (C) $15\times2\times\dfrac{1}{3}$

   (D) $2+\left(\dfrac{1}{3}\times15\right)$

   (E) $(2\times15)+\left(2\times\dfrac{1}{3}\right)$

$$\frac{1}{4}\,\square\,\frac{1}{2}=N$$

6. Which of the following symbols, when used in place of the box in the equation shown above, will result in the greatest value of N?

   (A) −
   (B) +
   (C) ×
   (D) ÷
   (E) The value of N will be the same for each of the symbols

Checkpoint Review

1. Patricia is working on a science project. She worked for $1\frac{1}{2}$ hours on Wednesday, $\frac{3}{4}$ hour on Thursday, and $2\frac{2}{3}$ hours on Saturday. How much time, in total hours, did Patricia spend working on the science project?

    (A) $3\frac{5}{6}$

    (B) $3\frac{11}{12}$

    (C) $4\frac{5}{6}$

    (D) $4\frac{11}{12}$

    (E) $5\frac{1}{6}$

    _____

2. What is the value of $5\frac{7}{8} - 3\frac{1}{4} + 3\frac{1}{2}$?

    (A) $5\frac{5}{8}$

    (B) $5\frac{3}{4}$

    (C) 6

    (D) $6\frac{1}{8}$

    (E) $6\frac{1}{4}$

    _____

3. Marcia began her exercise routine at 4:48 p.m. Her cardio exercises lasted for $\frac{1}{2}$ of an hour. Her weight lifting lasted for half as long as her cardio exercise. At what time did she finish her exercise routine?

    (A) 5:08 p.m.
    (B) 5:18 p.m.
    (C) 5:23 p.m.
    (D) 5:28 p.m.
    (E) 5:33 p.m.

Checkpoint Review

4. Which of the following fractions is equivalent to $\left(\dfrac{2}{3}\right)^2 + \dfrac{1}{6}$?

    (A) $\dfrac{5}{6}$

    (B) $\dfrac{2}{9}$

    (C) $\dfrac{4}{9}$

    (D) $\dfrac{7}{18}$

    (E) $\dfrac{11}{18}$

---

5. A store sold $\dfrac{1}{2}$ of its T.V.s on Monday, and $\dfrac{1}{8}$ of its remaining T.V.s on Tuesday. If 7 T.V.s remained, how many T.V.s did the store start with on Monday morning?

    (A) 6
    (B) 12
    (C) 16
    (D) 24
    (E) 32

---

6. At a peanut processing plant, $\dfrac{1}{5}$ of all raw peanuts that arrive at the facility are not suitable to be processed and sold. If 1,000 pounds of peanuts must be sold, how many pounds of raw peanuts should be received at the processing plant?

    (A) 1,100
    (B) 1,200
    (C) 1,250
    (D) 1,400
    (E) 1,500

Place Value

❑ **Decimals** are a way of writing fractions whose denominators are powers of 10.

$$\frac{4}{10} = .4 \qquad\qquad \frac{36}{1,000} = .036 \qquad\qquad \frac{1200}{10,000} = \underline{\hspace{2cm}}$$

❑ The position of each digit in a number determines the digit's **place value**.

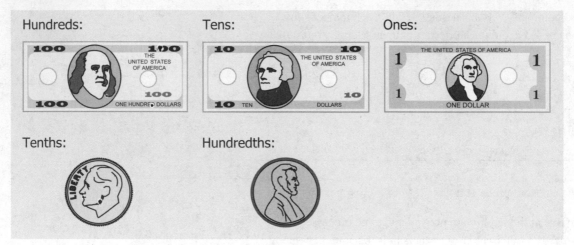

❑ It might help to think of money when working with decimals and place value.

TRY IT OUT

1. What digit is in the <u>hundredths</u> place in the number 536.187?

2. What digit is in the <u>hundreds</u> place in the number 536.187?

PUT IT TOGETHER

1. Which digit in the number 2,148.9 has the LEAST value?

    (A) 1
    (B) 2
    (C) 3
    (D) 4
    (E) 9

---

2. Which of the following is the number: three-hundred twelve and sixty-four thousandths?

    (A) 3,012.64
    (B) 3,012.064
    (C) 312.64
    (D) 312.064
    (E) 0.31264

---

3. How many thousandths are in 0.2?

    (A) 0.02
    (B) 2
    (C) 20
    (D) 200
    (E) 2000

---

4. How many tenths are in $5\frac{1}{2}$?

    (A) 52
    (B) 55
    (C) 505
    (D) 520
    (E) 550

Rounding & Estimation

❑ To round a number, look at the digit to the right of the place you're rounding to.

   If that digit is greater than or equal to 5, round up; if that digit is less than 5, round down.

> Round 942.637 to the nearest:
>
>   hundredth = 942.64
>
>   tenth = 942.6
>
>   whole number = 943
>
>   hundred = 900
>
>   thousand = 1,000

TRY IT OUT

1. Round 1.5 to the nearest whole number.

2. Round 1.54 to the nearest tenth.

3. Round 2.227 to the nearest hundredth.

4. Round 23.358 to the nearest whole number.

5. Round 351 to the nearest hundred.

6. Round 351 to the nearest ten.

7. Round 99.99 to the nearest tenth.

8. Which of the following is closest to $3,315 \div 3.3$?

   (A) 10
   (B) 100
   (C) 110
   (D) 1,000
   (E) 1,100

9. Which of the following is closest to $78,826 \div 2.09$?

   (A) 30,000
   (B) 35,000
   (C) 40,000
   (D) 45,000
   (E) 400,000

PUT IT TOGETHER

1. What will be the approximate price for 4 plates if they cost $1.47 each?

    (A) $5
    (B) $6
    (C) $7
    (D) $8
    (E) $9

    _____

2. Which sum is closest to $19 + 27 + 71$?

    (A) $20 + 30 + 70$
    (B) $20 + 20 + 70$
    (C) $20 + 90$
    (D) $40 + 70$
    (E) $30 + 70$

    _____

$$\frac{309}{1,256} =$$

3. The resulting quotient of the calculation shown above is closest to which of the following?

    (A) $\dfrac{2}{3}$

    (B) $\dfrac{1}{2}$

    (C) $\dfrac{1}{3}$

    (D) $\dfrac{1}{4}$

    (E) $\dfrac{1}{5}$

4. When 6,513 is divided by 407, the result is closest to which of the following?

    (A) 12
    (B) 13
    (C) 14
    (D) 15
    (E) 16

---

5. Peter spent a total of $28\frac{3}{4}$ hours working on a project, and he earned \$12.11 per hour. Of the following, which is closest to the total amount he earned for his work on the project?

    (A) \$400
    (B) \$360
    (C) \$300
    (D) \$250
    (E) \$240

Decimals

❑ To **add or subtract decimals**, line up the decimal points. Place the decimal point for your answer beneath the other decimal points. Do this **before** you add or subtract. Then add or subtract as you would any other set of numbers.

$$342 + 1.93 + 12.46 \Rightarrow \begin{array}{r} 342.00 \\ 1.93 \\ +\ \underline{12.46} \\ 356.39 \end{array}$$

❑ To **multiply decimals**, multiply the numbers as you would any other numbers. Then count the total number of decimal places in the numbers you are multiplying. Place the decimal in the product this many places from the right.

$$23.6 \times 1.9 = ? \quad \Rightarrow \quad \begin{array}{r} 236 \\ \times\ \underline{19} \\ 2124 \\ \underline{2360} \\ 4484 \end{array} \quad \Rightarrow \quad 4484.0 \quad \Rightarrow \quad 44.84$$

23.6 has one decimal place and 1.9 has one decimal place, so there is a

total of two decimal places. Therefore, we place the decimal in the

product two places from the right.

❑ To **divide by a decimal**, follow these steps:

1. Move the decimal point in the divisor to the right until you have a whole number.

2. Move the decimal point in the dividend the same number of places to the right.

3. Place a decimal point directly above the new decimal point in the dividend.

4. Divide.

TRY IT OUT

1. $1.0003 + 5.2 + 12.62 =$

2. $30.39 + 50.61 + 2 =$

3. $10 - 2.35 =$

4. $150.55 - 54 =$

5. $\dfrac{5}{10} + \dfrac{45}{100} =$

6. $28.1 \times .9 =$

7. $14 \times .07 =$

8. $1.4 \times .003 =$

9. $2.9 \times 1,000 =$

10. $.27 \times 12.2 =$

11. $\dfrac{9}{10} \times 100 =$

12. $.4\overline{)16}$

13. $.04\overline{)1.6}$

14. $.52\overline{)1.0452}$

15. $.001\overline{)16}$

16. $2.8\overline{)84.56}$

PUT IT TOGETHER

1. $0.0050 \times 10.00 =$

    (A) 5
    (B) 0.5
    (C) 0.05
    (D) 0.005
    (E) 0.0005

---

2. Half of the members in a group of 32 members contribute
    $0.15 each to a charity. How much was the total
    contribution of these members?

    (A) $48
    (B) $24
    (C) $4.80
    (D) $2.40
    (E) $0.48

Percent-Decimal-Fraction Conversion

❑ **Percents are hundredths**. Use this simple rule to convert percents to decimals or fractions.

19% ⟹ 19 hundredths ⟹ 0.19 or $\frac{19}{100}$

❑ To change a percent to a decimal, move the decimal point two places to the left. To change a decimal to a percent, move the decimal point two places to the right.

4% ⟹ 04.0% ⟹ .04

1.43 ⟹ 1.430 ⟹ 143.0%

❑ Percents are a way of expressing fractions with a denominator of 100.

To change a percent to a fraction, put the percent over 100 (without the percent sign). To change a fraction to a percent, change the fraction to an equivalent fraction with a denominator of 100.

25% ⟹ 25 out of 100 ⟹ $\frac{25}{100}$ ⟹ $\frac{1}{4}$

Convert $\frac{3}{5}$ to a percent.

$\frac{3}{5}$ ⟹ $\frac{3}{5} \times \frac{20}{20}$ ⟹ $\frac{60}{100}$ ⟹ 60%

❑ You can also change a fraction into a decimal by dividing the numerator by the denominator. Then change the resulting decimal to a percent.

Convert $\frac{4}{20}$ to a percent.

$\frac{4}{20}$ ⟹ $20\overline{)4.00}$ ⟹ .20 = 20%

TRY IT OUT

Express the following decimals as percents:

1. .63

2. 2.07

3. .04

4. 0.1256

5. .0005

Express the following percents as decimals:

6. 73%

7. 119%

8. $7\frac{1}{2}\%$

9. .75%

10. 2.1%

Convert the following percents to fractions:

11. 40%

12. 68 %

13. 8%

14. 140%

15. 1001%

Convert the following fractions to percents:

16. $\frac{1}{10}$

17. $\frac{1}{4}$

18. $\frac{3}{5}$

19. $1\frac{1}{5}$

20. $\frac{5}{7}$

PUT IT TOGETHER

1. All of the following expressions are equal to each other
    EXCEPT:

    (A) .3
    (B) $\dfrac{3}{10}$
    (C) $\dfrac{300}{1000}$
    (D) .300
    (E) 3%

---

2. Which of the following expressions is NOT equal to
    $1,600 \times 0.4$?

    (A) $1,600 \times \dfrac{4}{10}$
    (B) $1,600 \times \dfrac{4}{100}$
    (C) 160×4
    (D) 16×40
    (E) 1.6×400

---

3. If 20 out of 25 students in a school class went on a field
    trip, what percent of the total number of students went on
    the trip?

    (A) 95%
    (B) 80%
    (C) 75%
    (D) 25%
    (E) 20%

4. $\frac{1}{5}$ percent =

(A) 0.002
(B) 0.02
(C) 0.2
(D) 2
(E) 20

Percents

❑ Method 1: **"Is over of"** calls for a proportion. One side of the proportion is the percentage written as a fraction. The other side is a fraction in which the numerator is the number that comes after the word "is" and the denominator is the number that comes after the word "of."

$$\frac{is}{of} = \frac{percent}{100}$$

40% of what number is 16?

40% of what number   is 16?

denominator   numerator

$\dfrac{40}{100} = \dfrac{16}{x}$ ⇨   Cross-multiply to solve: $40x = 1600$ ⇨ $x = 40$

Note: "cross-multiplying" is covered later in the Proportions lesson.

❑ Method 2: **Translation** calls for translating the words in the question directly to a math equation.

40% of what number is 16?

40%   ⇨   0.4

of   ⇨   multiplication

what number   ⇨ n

is   ⇨   =

16   ⇨   16

40% of what number is 16?   ⇨ $(0.4) \times n = 16$

$(0.4) \times n = 16$ ⇨ $n = \dfrac{16}{0.4}$ ⇨   n = 40

TRY IT OUT

1. What is 40% of 12?

2. What is 25% of 250?

3. What is 8% of 16?

4. What is 150% of 30?

5. 12 is what percent of 24?

6. What percent of 48 is 36?

7. 50 is what percent of 40?

8. What percent of 210 is 70?

9. 10% of what number is 20?

10. 80% of what number is 5?

11. $33\frac{1}{3}$% of what number is 10?

12. 250% of what number is 5?

PUT IT TOGETHER

1. If 20 percent of N is 30, then 10 percent of the same number is

    (A) 10
    (B) 12
    (C) 15
    (D) 18
    (E) 20

2. 110 is 50% of what number?

    (A) 50
    (B) 55
    (C) 155
    (D) 200
    (E) 220

3. Stefan wants to buy 2 sandwiches that have a regular price of N dollars each. The shop that sells the sandwiches has a deal in which the second sandwich is half the regular price. If he buys the two sandwiches, what percent of the regular price of two sandwiches will he pay?

    (A) 25%
    (B) 50%
    (C) 75%
    (D) 100%
    (E) 125%

4. In a school club, 60% of the student members are girls. If there are 24 boys in the club, how many students are in the club?

    (A) 64
    (B) 60
    (C) 48
    (D) 40
    (E) 36

5. If 20 percent of a number is equal to x, which of the following is equal to 10 percent of twice the same number?

(A) $4x$

(B) $2x$

(C) x

(D) $\dfrac{x}{2}$

(E) $\dfrac{x}{4}$

6. The price of a computer is decreased by 50%. If this new price is increased by 50%, what will be the percent change from the original price of the computer to the final price?

(A) 25%

(B) 40%

(C) 50%

(D) 60%

(E) 100%

7. Harriet currently has $12,600 in her savings account. If her account receives 5 percent interest per year, how much did she have in her account one year ago?

(A) $13,230

(B) $13,200

(C) $12,030

(D) $12,000

(E) $11,970

Checkpoint Review

1. What is the hundreds digit in the largest 6-digit odd
    number that can be made if each of the digits 5, 8, 3, 0, 4,
    and 7 is used only once?

    (A) 3
    (B) 4
    (C) 5
    (D) 7
    (E) 8

2. What is 8% of 45% of 50?

    (A) 0.018
    (B) 0.18
    (C) 1.8
    (D) 18
    (E) 180

3. By accepting 40 more students, a school increased its total
    number of students by 25%. How many students did the
    school have after the increase?

    (A) 120
    (B) 160
    (C) 180
    (D) 200
    (E) 220

4. A bakery offered a discount of 35% on all of its goods for
    one week. After the sale ended, by what fraction of the
    discounted prices did the prices of goods increase?

    (A) $\frac{7}{20}$

    (B) $\frac{6}{13}$

    (C) $\frac{1}{2}$

    (D) $\frac{13}{20}$

    (E) $\frac{7}{13}$

Checkpoint Review

5. An electronics store is having a holiday sale with 50% off for all items. If the store also has coupons for an additional 60% off the sales price, what is the total percent that can be saved on the original price of items during the sale?

    (A) 110%
    (B) 90%
    (C) 80%
    (D) 70%
    (E) 30%

6. What percent of 3 hours is 43 minutes and 12 seconds?

    (A) 4%
    (B) 18%
    (C) 24%
    (D) 36%
    (E) 48%

7. Eduardo wants to buy a car that costs $13,500. There is an additional 6.25% sales tax added to the price of the car. What is the total cost, to the nearest cent, of the car after tax?

    (A) 12,705.88
    (B) 13,416.15
    (C) 13,584.38
    (D) 14,343.75
    (E) 21,937.50

Ratios

❑ When two quantities are compared by dividing one quantity by the other, the comparison is called a **ratio**.

A ratio may be written as "X:Y" or "X/Y" or "X to Y."

❑ A ratio can be thought of as a comparison of parts.

In a fruit basket, there are 3 oranges to every 2 apples.

The ratio of apples to oranges is 2:3.

If there are only apples and oranges in the basket, the ratio of apples to the whole basket is 2:5 and the ratio of oranges to the whole basket is 3:5.

❑ A ratio doesn't necessarily represent the actual number of things.

If the ratio of boys to girls in a class is 1:3, it means that for every boy in the class, there are 3 girls.

The ratio of boys to total students is 1:4. The ratio of girls to total students is 3:4.

If there are 20 students in the class, 5 of the students are boys and 15 of the students are girls. You can figure this by multiplying both terms in the ratio by 5.

TRY IT OUT

Express the following as ratios:

1. $4 to $7

2. 40 cm to 1m

3. 10 in. to 3 ft.

Solve the following word problems:

4. A class has 18 girls and 12 boys. What is the ratio of girls to boys?

5. A class has 15 girls and x boys. The ratio of girls to boys is 3:2. How many boys are in the class?

6. Ricky runs twice as fast as he jogs. If he can run a mile in 6 minutes, how many minutes will it take him to jog a mile?

7. A basket has apples and oranges. The ratio of apples to oranges is 1:4. If there are 24 oranges in the basket, how many of pieces of fruit are in the basket?

PUT IT TOGETHER

1. The ratio of 2 to 3 is the same as the ratio of all of the following EXCEPT

   (A) 6 to 8
   (B) 10 to 15
   (C) 12 to 18
   (D) 16 to 24
   (E) 18 to 27

2. Hannah runs half as fast as she rides her bicycle. If she runs to the library in 30 minutes, how many minutes does it take her to ride her bicycle to the library?

   (A) 15 minutes
   (B) 30 minutes
   (C) 40 minutes
   (D) 45 minutes
   (E) 60 minutes

3. The ratio of boys to girls in a classroom is 4 to 3. If there are 28 children in the classroom, how many are girls?

   (A) 7
   (B) 12
   (C) 16
   (D) 21
   (E) 24

4. In a basket of fruit, there are 32 apples for every 48 oranges. What is the ratio of apples to oranges?

   (A) 2:5
   (B) 3:5
   (C) 2:3
   (D) 3:2
   (E) 5:2

5. Justin has the same number of $5 bills as $10 bills. If the value of his $5 bills plus the value of his $10 bills equals $120, how many $5 bills does Justin have?

(A) 6
(B) 8
(C) 12
(D) 40
(E) 80

6. Gregory plants 16 trees in an orchard with an area of 4,000 square feet. He should only have two trees for every 800 square feet. How many trees should he remove from the orchard?

(A) 3
(B) 4
(C) 5
(D) 6
(E) 11

Proportions

❏ A proportion is a statement that two ratios are equivalent.

❏ The quickest way to solve proportions is usually to **cross-multiply**. With both ratios written as fractions, multiply the numerator of each ratio by the denominator of the other, and set the products equal to each other.

In other words, $\dfrac{a}{b} = \dfrac{c}{d}$ is a proportion if $ad = bc.$.

> Jon eats 2 hard-boiled eggs every 5 minutes. At this rate, how many hard-boiled eggs will Jon eat in 30 minutes?
>
> Let x = the number of hard-boiled eggs Jon will eat in 30 minutes.
>
> Now set up a proportion:
>
> $$\frac{2 \text{ eggs}}{5 \text{ minutes}} = \frac{x \text{ eggs}}{30 \text{ minutes}}$$
>
> Cross-multiply:
>
> $$\frac{2}{5} = \frac{x}{30} \implies \frac{2}{5} \diagup\!\!\!\!\diagdown \frac{x}{30} \implies 5 \cdot x = 2 \cdot 30 \implies 5x = 60 \implies x = 12$$

❏ Proportions can sometimes be solved by finding common denominators.

$$\frac{6}{15} = \frac{x}{10} \implies \frac{6}{15}\cdot\left(\frac{2}{2}\right) = \frac{x}{10}\cdot\left(\frac{3}{3}\right) \implies \frac{12}{30} = \frac{3x}{30} \implies x = 4$$

❏ **Dimensional analysis** is a method for converting between and among different units using conversion factors. Convert between units by multiplying by the units' conversion ratio. Set up the ratios so that your product is in the necessary unit and other units cancel. You may need to do multiple conversions to get the necessary unit.

> How many seconds are in 1.5 days?
>
> $$1.5 \text{ days} \times \frac{24 \text{ hours}}{1 \text{ day}} \times \frac{60 \text{ minutes}}{1 \text{ hour}} \times \frac{60 \text{ seconds}}{1 \text{ minute}} = 129{,}600 \text{ seconds}$$

> How many hours are in one week? _____

TRY IT OUT

Solve for *n*:

1. $\dfrac{n}{2} = \dfrac{4}{1}$

2. $\dfrac{5}{6} = \dfrac{n}{12}$

3. $\dfrac{2}{3} = \dfrac{8}{n}$

4. $\dfrac{n}{10} = \dfrac{8}{5}$

5. $\dfrac{5}{n} = \dfrac{6}{10}$

Solve the following word problems:

6. If a dealer buys 24 pairs of shoes for $300, how much does he pay for a shipment of 36 pairs of shoes at the same rate?

7. If Frank needs to feed his kittens 5 ounces of milk every 2 hours, how many ounces does he use in one day?

8. A map is drawn to a scale of 10 miles = 1 inch. What distance is represented by 2.5 inches?

9. A motorist used 8 gallons of gasoline to travel 160 miles. At the same rate, how many gallons of gas does the motorist need to travel 80 miles?

PUT IT TOGETHER

1. If $\dfrac{4}{3n} = \dfrac{1}{9}$, then $n =$

    (A) 12
    (B) 16
    (C) 18
    (D) 24
    (E) 36

---

2. If 10 biscuits cost \$2, then, at the same rate, a dozen biscuits will cost

    (A) \$2.20
    (B) \$2.40
    (C) \$2.80
    (D) \$3.00
    (E) \$3.60

---

3. Barry solved 2 math problems in 30 minutes. At the same rate, how long will it take him to solve 11 math problems?

    (A) 2 hours 15 minutes
    (B) 2 hours 30 minutes
    (C) 2 hours 45 minutes
    (D) 3 hours
    (E) 3 hours 15 minutes

---

4. On a blueprint, a line 4 inches long represents 32 feet. On this blueprint, how many inches represent 80 feet?

    (A) 10
    (B) 12
    (C) 14
    (D) 15
    (E) 16

5. Approximately how many centimeters are in 90 inches?
    (1 meter = 3.28 feet)

    (A) 2.3
    (B) 2.46
    (C) 24.6
    (D) 228.7
    (E) 2460.0

---

6. A train travels at a speed of 2000 meters per minute.
    What is the train's approximate speed in miles per hour?
    (1.61 kilometer = 1 mile)

    (A) 745
    (B) 192
    (C) 75
    (D) 19
    (E) 8

Order of Operations

❑ To simplify a problem with multiple operations, you need to follow the order of operations.

1. Parentheses: ( )

2. Exponents: 3^2

3. Multiplication: 2×4

4. Division: $6 \div 2$

5. Addition: $5 + 6$

6. Subtraction: $9 - 6$

Simplify:

$3 \times (10 - 2) - 7 + 4^2 =$

$\qquad = 3 \times 8 - 7 + 4^2$ (parentheses)

$\qquad = 3 \times 8 - 7 + 16$ (exponents)

$\qquad = 24 - 7 + 16$ (multiplication)

$\qquad = 17 + 16$ (addition / subtraction)

$\qquad = 33$ (addition)

$5 \times 4 + 3 - 2 =$ _____

$5 \times 4 + (3 - 2) =$ _____

$5 \times (4 + 3) - 2 =$ _____

$5 \times (4 + 3 - 2) =$ _____

Just remember "**P**lease **E**xcuse **M**y **D**ear **A**unt **S**ally" or the word **PEMDAS** and you'll remember the order of operations.

Note: Addition does not necessarily come before subtraction. When you get to the addition and subtraction part of the simplification, move from left to right through the expression.

TRY IT OUT

Simplify:

1. $9 \times 2^2 + 3 - \left(2^3 - 6\right) =$

2. $15 \div 3 + 2 \times (2-1)^2 =$

3. $12^2 + 4^3 - \dfrac{6^2}{3} =$

4. $\left(7 - (2+2+2)\right)^2 =$

PUT IT TOGETHER

1. $4 \times (2 + 2 \times 4) =$

   (A) 16
   (B) 20
   (C) 32
   (D) 40
   (E) 64

   ---

2. The expression $\sqrt{49} \times \left(3n^2 + n^2\right) - 2$ is equal to

   (A) $28n^2 - 2$
   (B) $26n^2$
   (C) $21n^4 - 2$
   (D) $11n^4 - 2$
   (E) $9n^2$

Sequences, Patterns, & Logic

❑ To compare the relative sizes of decimals, line up the decimal points.

> List the following numbers from smallest to largest: 0.27, 2.85, 28.6, 0.271.
>
> Arrange the numbers vertically and keep the decimal points in one line:
>
> 0.27
>
> 2.85
>
> 28.6
>
> 0.271
>
> Since 28.6 is the only number with a tens place, it is the largest.
>
> 2.85 is the next largest.
>
> 0.27 is the same as 0.270, which is smaller than .271.
>
> So, from smallest to largest, the numbers go: 0.27, 0.271, 2.85, 28.6

❑ To compare the relative sizes of fractions, find the lowest common denominator and compare the numerators.

❑ **Consecutive numbers** are whole numbers that increase or decrease incrementally by 1.

> $\{4,5,6\}$ and $\{9,8,7,6,5\}$ are both sets of consecutive numbers.
>
> $\{n, n+1, n+2, n+3\}$ is also a set of consecutive numbers.

❑ Sequences and patterns can often be solved by recognizing trends or by writing out the numbers.

> The price of a single doughnut is $0.79, and the price of each additional doughnut is 2 cents less than the previous one. If Doug buys 5 doughnuts, what is the price of his fifth doughnut?
>
> 1st = $0.79, 2nd = $0.77, 3rd = $0.75, 4th = $0.73, 5th = $0.71

TRY IT OUT

1. List the following from largest to smallest:
    4.23, 33.1, 33.01, 4.1937, .00936.

2. List the following from largest to smallest: $\dfrac{2}{3}, \dfrac{3}{5}, \dfrac{5}{12}, \dfrac{7}{10}$

3. Donna is taller than Theodore but shorter than William. Theodore is taller than Fred but shorter than Regina. Who is shortest?

4. The sum of a pair of consecutive numbers is 39. What is the smaller of the two numbers?

PUT IT TOGETHER

1. Which of the following numbers is the smallest?

    (A) 0

    (B) $-\dfrac{1}{10}$

    (C) 1

    (D) $\dfrac{1}{10}$

    (E) -1

---

2. Buck is younger than Jim but older than Maddie. Maddie is older than Graham. Who is youngest?

    (A) Buck
    (B) Graham
    (C) Jim
    (D) Maddie
    (E) It cannot be determined from the information given.

---

3. A history textbook has a picture on the third page and on every second page after the third. No other pages in the book have pictures. Which of the following is the number of a page that will have a picture?

    (A) 11
    (B) 12
    (C) 14
    (D) 20
    (E) 30

---

4. On a shelf, gems are placed in this repeating pattern: pink, blue, green, yellow, red; pink, blue, green, yellow, red; etc. If the first gem is pink, what will be the color of the 63rd gem on the shelf?

    (A) blue
    (B) green
    (C) pink
    (D) red
    (E) yellow

5. The sum of three consecutive numbers is 204. What is the
    largest of the three numbers?

    (A) 615
    (B) 206
    (C) 69
    (D) 67
    (E) 66

Checkpoint Review

1. Trish is standing next to a telephone pole. Trish is 6 feet tall and her shadow is 20 feet long. If the pole casts a shadow with a length of 106 feet and 8 inches, what is the height, in feet, of the telephone pole?

   (A) 24
   (B) 30
   (C) 32
   (D) 36
   (E) 40

2. Amir can run 300 meters in 45 seconds. Which of the following is closest to Amir's running speed in miles per hour? (1 kilometer = 0.62 mile)

   (A) 2.5
   (B) 14.9
   (C) 24.0
   (D) 24.8
   (E) 38.7

3. A machine can produce 4 bottles every $\frac{3}{4}$ of a minute. At this rate, how many bottles can this machine produce in half an hour?

   (A) 40
   (B) 80
   (C) 160
   (D) 320
   (E) 640

Checkpoint Review

4. What is the value of $-(19-45)\div 6-(-4)^2\times(-1)$?

(A) $-20\dfrac{1}{3}$

(B) $-12\dfrac{1}{3}$

(C) $-11\dfrac{1}{3}$

(D) $11\dfrac{1}{3}$

(E) $20\dfrac{1}{3}$

---

5. 8, 9, 5, 3, 8, 9, 5, 3, …

In the sequence shown above, 8 is the first term and the pattern 8, 9, 5, 3 repeats itself indefinitely. Which of the following terms has a value of 5?

(A) 90th
(B) 91st
(C) 92nd
(D) 93rd
(E) 94th

Chapter Review

❏ Addition, Subtraction, Multiplication, & Division

On SSAT math problems, you will have to calculate sums, differences, products, and quotients.

❏ Odd & Even Integers

An odd number is an integer that is not divisible by 2. An even number is an integer that is divisible by 2.

❏ Positive & Negative Numbers

A positive number is any number that is greater than 0. A negative number is any number that is less than 0.

❏ Divisibility & Remainders

A number is divisible by another number if it can be evenly divided by that number with no remainder. When a number does not divide evenly into another number, the number that remains at the end of the division is called the remainder.

❏ Multiples & Factors

A multiple is the product of a particular number and another number. A factor of a number is a number that divides evenly into that number.

❏ Fractions

Fractions are used to represent portions of a whole. Fractions are written as $\dfrac{\text{PART}}{\text{WHOLE}}$.

To add or subtract fractions, first adjust the fractions so they have a common denominator. To multiply fractions, multiply straight across.

Two numbers are reciprocals if their product is 1. To find the reciprocal of a fraction, "flip" the fraction by switching its numerator and denominator.

❏ Place Value

Decimals are a way of writing fractions whose denominators are powers of 10. The position of each digit in a number determines the digit's place value.

❑ Rounding & Estimation

To round a number, look at the digit to the right of the place you're rounding to. If that digit is greater than or equal to 5, round up; if that digit is less than 5, round down.

❑ Percents

"Is over of" calls for a proportion. One side of the proportion is the percentage written as a fraction. The other side is a fraction in which the numerator is the number that comes after the word "is" and the denominator is the number that comes after the word "of."

❑ Ratios

When two quantities are compared by dividing one quantity by the other, the comparison is called a ratio. A ratio may be written as "X:Y" or "X/Y" or "X to Y."

❑ Proportions

A proportion is a statement that two ratios are equivalent. The quickest way to solve proportions is usually to cross-multiply. With both ratios written as fractions, multiply the numerator of each ratio by the denominator of the other, and set the products equal to each other. In other words, $\frac{a}{b} = \frac{c}{d}$ is a proportion if $ad = bc$.

❑ Order of Operations

To simplify a problem with multiple operations, you need to follow the order of operations.

1. Parentheses: ( )

2. Exponents: 3^2

3. Multiplication: 2×4

4. Division: $6 \div 2$

5. Addition: $5 + 6$

6. Subtraction: $9 - 6$

❑ Sequences, Patterns, & Logic

To compare the relative sizes of decimals, line up the decimal points. To compare the relative sizes of fractions, find the lowest common denominator and compare the numerators. Consecutive numbers are whole numbers that increase or decrease incrementally by 1. Sequences and patterns can often be solved by recognizing trends or by writing out the numbers.

Number Concepts & Operations Practice

Addition, Subtraction, Multiplication, & Division

1. $1,000 - 32 =$

(A) 1032
(B) 972
(C) 971
(D) 970
(E) 968

2.   John's term paper is 10,000 words long. If he has typed only 1,564 of those words so far, how many words does he have left to type?

(A) 8,336
(B) 8,436
(C) 8,454
(D) 8,546
(E) 9,536

3.   If $50 - y = 50$, then $50y =$

(A) -50
(B) 0
(C) $\frac{1}{50}$
(D) 1
(E) 10

4. $4 \times 3 \times 2 \times 1 \times 0 = ?$

(A) 24
(B) 10
(C) 5
(D) 1
(E) 0

5.   If $N \times N \times N = 1$, then $N =$

(A) 1/3
(B) 1/2
(C) 1
(D) 3/2
(E) 2

Odd & Even Integers

6. Which of the following is an odd integer that is between 3 and 8 and between 6 and 11?

    (A) 5
    (B) 6
    (C) 6.5
    (D) 7
    (E) 8

7. If N is the sum of two odd integers, then which of the following is always true?

    (A) N is positive
    (B) N is negative
    (C) N is even
    (D) N is odd
    (E) N is greater than both numbers

8. If $18 \times w$ is an even integer, then w can be

    (A) 2
    (B) 3
    (C) 6
    (D) 7
    (E) all of the above

9. If n is an even integer, which of the following must be an odd integer?

    (A) $n \div 2$
    (B) $3n$
    (C) $2n + 1$
    (D) $n - 2$
    (E) $2n$

10. If N is an integer, and $3(N + 1)$ is even, which of the following CANNOT be true?

    (A) N is odd
    (B) N is even
    (C) $N + 1$ is even
    (D) N is negative
    (E) $3N + 3$ is even

Positive & Negative Numbers

11. $-2 \times 7 \times -3 \div -6 =$

    (A) -7
    (B) -6
    (C) -2
    (D) 2
    (E) 7

12. The temperature at 5 a.m. was 6 degrees below zero. If the temperature rose 11 degrees by 1 p.m., then the temperature at 1 p.m. was

    (A) 17 degrees above zero
    (B) 8 degrees above zero
    (C) 5 degrees above zero
    (D) 1 degree below zero
    (E) 17 degrees below zero

13. If L is a non-zero whole number, then $L \times (L + 1)$ is always

    (A) odd
    (B) even
    (C) 0
    (D) negative
    (E) positive

Divisibility & Remainders

14. Eric has 24 checkers. If he divides the checkers into 3 equal groups, how many checkers are in each group?

    (A) 5
    (B) 6
    (C) 7
    (D) 8
    (E) 9

15. If $7 \div 5 = d$ with a remainder of 2, what is d?

    (A) 0
    (B) 1
    (C) 2
    (D) 5
    (E) 7

16. If $419 \div 10 = 41$ with a remainder of R, what is R?

    (A) 2
    (B) 3
    (C) 5
    (D) 7
    (E) 9

17. When N is divided by 4, the remainder is 2. What is the remainder when N is divided by 2?

    (A) 4
    (B) 3
    (C) 2
    (D) 1
    (E) 0

18. If x is divisible by 4, which of the following statements must always be true?

    (A) $x + 2$ is divisible by 2
    (B) $x + 2$ is divisible by 3
    (C) $x + 2$ is divisible by 4
    (D) $x + 2$ is divisible by 5
    (E) $x + 2$ is divisible by 6

Multiples & Factors

19. Mrs. Flynn bought 5 dozen cookies for her students. Mrs. Flynn has 20 students in her class. What is the greatest number of cookies that each student may have if the cookies are shared equally?

    (A) 3
    (B) 5
    (C) 7
    (D) 12
    (E) 20

20. After the tickets for a show were sold, $140 had been collected. If all the tickets were the same price, which of the following CANNOT be the price for one ticket?

    (A) $1.40
    (B) $2.00
    (C) $6.00
    (D) $7.00
    (E) $10.00

21. Alex has three times as many dresses as skirts. Which of the following could be the sum of her dresses and skirts?

    (A) 6
    (B) 7
    (C) 10
    (D) 12
    (E) 15

22. What is the least common multiple of 8, 9, and 30?

    (A) 120
    (B) 240
    (C) 360
    (D) 720
    (E) 2160

23. P is a prime number less than 9. Which of the following CANNOT be P?

    (A) 2
    (B) 3
    (C) 4
    (D) 5
    (E) 7

Fractions

24. $56 - 7\frac{2}{5} =$

    (A) $48\frac{2}{5}$

    (B) $48\frac{3}{5}$

    (C) $49\frac{2}{5}$

    (D) $49\frac{3}{5}$

    (E) $64\frac{2}{5}$

---

25. $1 + \frac{1}{2}$ is greater than which of the following?

    (A) $\frac{2}{2}$

    (B) $\frac{3}{2}$

    (C) $\frac{4}{2}$

    (D) $\frac{5}{2}$

    (E) $\frac{6}{2}$

---

26. $\frac{1}{4} \times 48 \times \frac{1}{3} \times 12 =$

    (A) 12

    (B) 16

    (C) 40

    (D) 48

    (E) 56

27. At a clothing store, $\frac{2}{5}$ of the shirts on sale are medium

size and $\frac{1}{6}$ of the shirts on sale are large size. What

fraction of the shirts on sale are not medium or large size?

(A) $\frac{13}{30}$

(B) $\frac{14}{30}$

(C) $\frac{15}{30}$

(D) $\frac{16}{30}$

(E) $\frac{17}{30}$

28. Nora has traveled $\frac{2}{7}$ of the way from her work to her

home. If Nora has been traveling for 8 minutes and travels
at a constant rate, how much longer, in minutes, will she
have to travel before she reaches her home?

(A) 20
(B) 22
(C) 24
(D) 26
(E) 28

29. Each of the following has the same value EXCEPT

(A) $3 \div \frac{1}{2}$

(B) $4 \div \frac{2}{3}$

(C) $8 \div \frac{4}{3}$

(D) $9 \div \frac{2}{3}$

(E) $15 \div \frac{5}{2}$

30. Lawrence bought a container with 64 ounces of milk. For different recipes, he used the following amounts, in ounces, of milk from his container: $2\frac{1}{2}$, $6\frac{2}{3}$, $10\frac{3}{4}$, and $4\frac{2}{3}$. How much milk, in ounces, does Lawrence have remaining in his container?

(A) $38\frac{7}{12}$

(B) $39\frac{5}{12}$

(C) $39\frac{7}{12}$

(D) $41\frac{5}{12}$

(E) $41\frac{7}{12}$

31. Kristal is making cookies and muffins for a bake sale. She has a recipe for a dozen cookies and another recipe for a dozen muffins. The amount of white sugar and brown sugar needed for each recipe is shown in the table below.

Sugar Needed		
Type of Sugar	Brown	White
12 Cookies	$\frac{3}{4}$ cup	$\frac{1}{2}$ cup
12 Muffins	$\frac{2}{3}$ cup	$\frac{1}{2}$ cup

If Kristal wants to make 3 dozen muffins and 2 dozen cookies, what is the total amount of sugar, in cups, needed?

(A) $2\frac{5}{12}$

(B) 6

(C) $6\frac{1}{12}$

(D) $7\frac{1}{4}$

(E) $14\frac{1}{6}$

Place Value

32. What is the hundreds digit in the number 67,675?

    (A) 600
    (B) 70
    (C) 6
    (D) 7
    (E) 5

33. Which of the following is 90,603?

    (A) nine thousand six hundred three
    (B) nineteen thousand sixty-three
    (C) ninety thousand six hundred three
    (D) nine hundred thousand sixty-three
    (E) nine hundred thousand six hundred three

34. What is the units digit of $5 \times 5 \times 5$?

    (A) 0
    (B) 1
    (C) 3
    (D) 5
    (E) 7

Rounding & Estimation

35. What is the best estimate for $9,887 \times 1,001$?

    (A) 99,000
    (B) 980,000
    (C) 990,000
    (D) 9,800,000
    (E) 9,900,000

36. Which of the following is closest to 0.24×105?

    (A) 2 times 10.5
    (B) half of 100
    (C) half of 210
    (D) $\frac{1}{4}$ of 100
    (E) $\frac{1}{4}$ of 111

Decimals

37. $0.1 + 0.01 + 0.001$ is equal to

 (A) .101
 (B) .101001
 (C) .1
 (D) .111
 (E) .3

___

38. Which of the following is closest to 5?

 (A) 4.9
 (B) 5.1
 (C) 5.01
 (D) 5.001
 (E) 5.0001

___

39. $0.0035 \times 4.00 =$

 (A) 140
 (B) 14.0
 (C) 1.4
 (D) 0.0140
 (E) 0.00140

___

40. X is equal to $\dfrac{2.8}{100}$. $10X$ is closest to which of the

 following?

 (A) 0.2
 (B) 0.3
 (C) 2.8
 (D) 28
 (E) 30

Percents

41. If Eliza has eaten 3 of the 10 cookies her father made, what percent of the cookies has she eaten?

    (A) 20%
    (B) 25%
    (C) 30%
    (D) 31%
    (E) 33%

42. Fred sells cars for Wreck-A-Week. There are 30 cars in the Wreck-A-Week lot. If Fred sold 20% of the cars in the lot, how many cars did he sell?

    (A) 6
    (B) 10
    (C) 12
    (D) 20
    (E) 24

43. 4 is 20% of

    (A) 5
    (B) 10
    (C) 16
    (D) 18
    (E) 20

44. 30% of $N =$

    (A) $3N$
    (B) $30N$
    (C) 15% of $2N$
    (D) $\dfrac{3}{100} \times N$
    (E) $\dfrac{1}{3} \times N$

SUMMIT
EDUCATIONAL
GROUP

45. If $y = 47$, then 10% of $10y = ?$

    (A) 4.7
    (B) 47
    (C) 50
    (D) 147
    (E) 470

46. If 20 is 60% of X, then 20 is 30% of what?

    (A) X
    (B) $2X$
    (C) $3X$
    (D) $4X$
    (E) $6X$

47. If 50% of X is 20, what is 25% of X?

    (A) 5
    (B) 10
    (C) 20
    (D) 40
    (E) 100

Ratios

48. There are twice as many goldfish as guppies in Sue's fish tank. If there are only goldfish and guppies in the fish tank, then which could be the total number of fish in the tank?

    (A) 5
    (B) 10
    (C) 15
    (D) 20
    (E) 25

49. At a dude ranch, there are three times as many horses walking around as there are humans. If there are 8 human legs at the ranch, how many horses are there?

    (A) 12
    (B) 24
    (C) 32
    (D) 48
    (E) 96

Proportions

50. Frederick is bicycling 3 miles every 20 minutes. At that rate, how many miles does he bicycle in 2 hours?

    (A) 6
    (B) 12
    (C) 15
    (D) 18
    (E) 24

51. In a recent university poll, there were 4.5 teachers for every 60 students. If there are 12,000 students, how many teachers are there?

    (A) 9
    (B) 90
    (C) 900
    (D) 9,000
    (E) 90,000

Order of Operations

52. $2(4 - 6) - (-8 + 2) \div 3 =$

(A) -10
(B) -6
(C) -2
(D) $\dfrac{2}{3}$
(E) 6

Sequences, Patterns, & Logic

53. Susan is twice as old as Bobby. Bobby is twice as old as William. If William is 5 years old, how old is Susan?

(A) 25
(B) 20
(C) 15
(D) 10
(E) 5

54. Ed is 2 inches taller than Ernie. Ernie is 2 inches shorter than Andrew. If Andrew is 59 inches tall, how tall is Ed?

(A) 59 inches
(B) 57 inches
(C) 55 inches
(D) 53 inches
(E) 51 inches

55. The smallest of 5 consecutive odd integers is 21. What is the average of the 5 integers?

(A) 19
(B) 22
(C) 23
(D) 25
(E) 30

Number Concepts & Operations Practice –

Middle Level

1. 3 friends painted a house together and earned a total of
    $600. If they split the earnings evenly, how much money
    did each friend get?

    (A) $50
    (B) $125
    (C) $150
    (D) $200
    (E) $300

2. $5,010 - 1,777 =$

    (A) 2,233
    (B) 3,233
    (C) 3,333
    (D) 3,343
    (E) 4,343

3. Which of the following is a true statement?

    (A) $10 \div 0 = 1$
    (B) $10 \div 1 = 1$
    (C) $10 \times 1 = 1$
    (D) $10 \div 10 = 1$
    (E) $10 \times 0 = 10$

4. A furniture factory makes stools with 3 legs and stools
    with 4 legs. At the end of one day, the number of 3-legged
    stools made is 16 and the number of 4-legged stools made
    is 12. Which is the total number of stool legs used by the
    factory at the end of that day?

    (A) 96
    (B) 86
    (C) 48
    (D) 28
    (E) It cannot be determined from the information given.

5.   In the figure above, what fraction of the fish have dark-colored tails?

(A) $\dfrac{1}{12}$

(B) $\dfrac{1}{9}$

(C) $\dfrac{1}{6}$

(D) $\dfrac{1}{3}$

(E) $\dfrac{1}{2}$

---

6.   Which of the following is NOT prime?

(A) 3
(B) 8
(C) 13
(D) 17
(E) 31

---

7.   John can do 50 jumping jacks in one minute. Jane can do 1 more jumping jack per minute than John can. How many jumping jacks can Jane do in two minutes?

(A) 50
(B) 100
(C) 101
(D) 102
(E) 200

8. Fred went to bed at 9:00 PM and got up for school at 6:00
    AM. How many hours did he sleep?

    (A) 2
    (B) 3
    (C) 6
    (D) 9
    (E) 12

9. Mary has to sell one carton of candy bars for her youth
    group fundraiser. She sold one-half of the candy bars in
    the carton and then ate two of them. If a carton contains
    24 candy bars, how many does Mary have left to sell?

    (A) 13
    (B) 12
    (C) 11
    (D) 10
    (E) 8

10. $\dfrac{7}{8} - \dfrac{1}{4} = ?$

    (A) 1

    (B) $\dfrac{5}{8}$

    (C) $\dfrac{3}{8}$

    (D) $\dfrac{1}{4}$

    (E) $\dfrac{1}{8}$

11. There are 6 packages of hamburger in the freezer. Each
    package weighs 1.5 pounds. How many pounds of
    hamburger are in the freezer?

    (A) 1.5 pounds
    (B) 4 pounds
    (C) 6 pounds
    (D) 7.5 pounds
    (E) 9 pounds

12. Which of the following is NOT true?

   (A) $\dfrac{1}{2} = \dfrac{2}{4}$

   (B) $\dfrac{1}{2} = \dfrac{3}{6}$

   (C) $\dfrac{1}{2} = \dfrac{4}{8}$

   (D) $\dfrac{1}{2} = \dfrac{5}{10}$

   (E) $\dfrac{1}{2} = \dfrac{6}{11}$

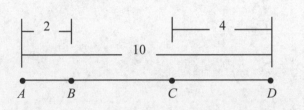

13. According to the figure above, what is the length of AC?

   (A) 4
   (B) 6
   (C) 8
   (D) 10
   (E) 12

14. $\dfrac{1}{7} \times \dfrac{1}{4} = ?$

   (A) $\dfrac{1}{28}$

   (B) $\dfrac{1}{11}$

   (C) $\dfrac{2}{11}$

   (D) $\dfrac{4}{7}$

   (E) $\dfrac{7}{4}$

15. Peter and Pam went to the supermarket. Peter bought $\frac{1}{2}$ pound of bologna. Pam bought $\frac{3}{4}$ pound of bologna. How much bologna did they buy?

(A) $1\frac{1}{4}$ pounds

(B) 1 pound

(C) 2 pounds

(D) $\frac{2}{3}$ pound

(E) $\frac{3}{8}$ pound

---

16. $\frac{1}{2} \times \frac{1}{2} \times \frac{1}{2} = ?$

(A) $\frac{3}{2}$

(B) $\frac{3}{6}$

(C) $\frac{1}{8}$

(D) $\frac{1}{6}$

(E) $\frac{1}{4}$

---

17. Jamie invited 20 friends to her birthday party. If $\frac{3}{5}$ of her guests are girls, how many of her guests are girls?

(A) 4

(B) 6

(C) 8

(D) 10

(E) 12

18. Karen has 9 quarters. If she buys 3 candy bars at 50 cents each, how many quarters does she have left?

(A) 0
(B) 1
(C) 2
(D) 3
(E) 4

19. Marty has 80 dimes. If he exchanges them for one-dollar bills, how many dollar bills will he receive?

(A) 4
(B) 5
(C) 6
(D) 7
(E) 8

20. John gave half of his candy bar to his little brother. John then ate half of what was left. What fraction of the candy bar did John eat?

(A) $\dfrac{3}{4}$

(B) $\dfrac{2}{3}$

(C) $\dfrac{1}{2}$

(D) $\dfrac{1}{3}$

(E) $\dfrac{1}{4}$

21. One can of beans weighs 14 ounces. How much will 5 cans of beans weigh?

(A) 90 ounces
(B) 80 ounces
(C) 70 ounces
(D) 60 ounces
(E) 50 ounces

22. $10\dfrac{1}{4} - 2\dfrac{3}{4} =$

(A) 8.25
(B) 8
(C) 7.75
(D) 7.5
(E) 7.25

23. Krista has 7 marbles and Jose has 15 marbles. How many marbles must Jose give Krista for each one to have the same number of marbles?

(A) 4
(B) 7
(C) 8
(D) 10
(E) 15

24. $3 \times \dfrac{2}{3}$ equals

(A) $10 \times \dfrac{2}{5}$

(B) $\dfrac{2}{3} \times \dfrac{3}{2}$

(C) $\dfrac{3}{2} \times \dfrac{4}{3}$

(D) $\dfrac{10}{5} \times \dfrac{5}{3}$

(E) $\dfrac{1}{3} \times \dfrac{6}{3}$

25. $\dfrac{12 + 8 + 4}{2 \times 4 \times 8} =$

(A) $\dfrac{3}{8}$

(B) $\dfrac{2}{5}$

(C) $\dfrac{3}{2}$

(D) $\dfrac{12}{7}$

(E) 6

26. A $15 pair of earrings is on sale for 20% off. What is the sale price of the earrings?

    (A) $3
    (B) $10
    (C) $12
    (D) $13
    (E) $14

27. A building has 47 floors, the first 7 of which are below the lobby. If an elevator starts on the third floor and goes 6 floors up, which of the following best describes where the elevator is now?

    (A) 2 floors below the lobby
    (B) the lobby
    (C) 1 floor above the lobby
    (D) 2 floors above the lobby
    (E) 9 floors above the lobby

28. Pat buys a piece of licorice 150 inches long. If she plans to give away all of the licorice by giving each of her 5 friends an equal piece, how long should she cut each piece?

    (A) 60 feet
    (B) 30 feet
    (C) 10 feet
    (D) 5 feet
    (E) 2.5 feet

29. $0.1 \times 10 \times 0.2 \times 5 =$

    (A) .5
    (B) 1
    (C) 1.5
    (D) 10
    (E) 50

30. What is the best estimate for $\dfrac{759,987}{1,998}$?

    (A) 40
    (B) 280
    (C) 400
    (D) 500
    (E) 4,000

31. Which of the following is equal to $2\overline{)178}$?

    (A) $\dfrac{178}{2}$

    (B) $178 \div 2$

    (C) $\dfrac{100}{2} + \dfrac{70}{2} + \dfrac{8}{2}$

    (D) 89

    (E) All of the above.

32. All the following are greater than $\dfrac{1}{2}$ except

    (A) $\dfrac{13}{25}$

    (B) $\dfrac{19}{39}$

    (C) $\dfrac{22}{43}$

    (D) $\dfrac{25}{49}$

    (E) $\dfrac{29}{54}$

33. If 30 percent of N is equal to $30, what is the value of N?

    (A) $1

    (B) $10

    (C) $100

    (D) $1,000

    (E) $10,000

34. If $\dfrac{1}{3}$ of a number is greater than 15, the number must be:

    (A) greater than 45

    (B) equal to 45

    (C) less than 45

    (D) equal to 5

    (E) less than 5

35. The price of gas dropped from $1.52 / gallon to
    $1.02 / gallon. This decrease is closest to what percent?

    (A) 10%
    (B) 13%
    (C) 15%
    (D) 33%
    (E) 40%

36. 977 runners began a marathon. If 30% of the runners did
    not finish, what is the best estimate of those who finished
    the race?

    (A) 270
    (B) 300
    (C) 600
    (D) 700
    (E) 937

37. Matt paid an additional $4.50 in tax for a meal that cost
    $45.00. What was the percent tax?

    (A) 1%
    (B) 2%
    (C) 5%
    (D) 10%
    (E) 11%

38. 36 is less than $\frac{3}{4}$ of a number. The number must be

    (A) less than 27
    (B) less than 48
    (C) equal to 108
    (D) greater than 48
    (E) greater than 72

39. All of the students at Small Town High play baseball or basketball, but not both. If there are twice as many students on the baseball team as on the basketball team, which of the following could be the number of students who go to Small Town High?

(A) 16
(B) 17
(C) 28
(D) 30
(E) 40

40. 201.86×9.75 is closest to which of the following?

(A) 200
(B) 450
(C) 1,800
(D) 2,000
(E) 2,100

41. Which is the largest fraction?

(A) $\dfrac{4}{7}$

(B) $\dfrac{5}{9}$

(C) $\dfrac{7}{15}$

(D) $\dfrac{9}{19}$

(E) $\dfrac{10}{21}$

42. At 4 a.m., the temperature was 12 degrees below 0. By 1 p.m., the temperature had risen 27 degrees. What was the temperature at 1 p.m.?

(A) 27 above zero
(B) 15 above zero
(C) 15 below zero
(D) 39 above zero
(E) 39 below zero

43. Which of the following is the largest?

    (A) 60% of 125
    (B) 30% of 125
    (C) 30% of 375
    (D) 60% of 250
    (E) 30% of 250

44. If the average of 7 consecutive whole numbers is 8, what is the largest number?

    (A) 11
    (B) 15
    (C) 16
    (D) 28
    (E) 56

45. Between 7 a.m. and 9:30 a.m., Carl makes 8 deliveries. If Carl keeps up this rate (with the exception of a lunch break between 1:00 p.m. and 1:30 p.m.), how many total deliveries will he make before finishing work at 3 p.m.?

    (A) 21
    (B) 24
    (C) 27
    (D) 29
    (E) 30

46. 75% of the 19,950 people who ride the subway drink coffee. The rest do not. What is the best approximation of those who DO NOT drink coffee?

    (A) 3,000
    (B) 5,000
    (C) 15,000
    (D) 17,000
    (E) 18,000

47. Donald Mac's restaurant has served 2.7 million customers. If King Burger's restaurant has served 220,000 fewer customers, how many customers has King Burger served?

   (A) 490,000
   (B) 2,480,000
   (C) 2,520,000
   (D) 2,920,000
   (E) 4,900,000

48. When Kelly drives to work, she has two travel expenses: parking and paying tolls. She must pay $1.50 in tolls each way (going to work and returning home) and $6 for parking. For every $42 Kelly spends in parking, how much does she spend on tolls?

   (A) $10.50
   (B) $21.00
   (C) $23.00
   (D) $63.00
   (E) $67.50

49. A contractor has 25 stories left to build on a building, which is now 13 stories less than the building next door to it. When finished, the new building will have

   (A) 12 more stories than the building next door
   (B) 38 fewer stories than the building next door
   (C) 12 fewer stories than the building next door
   (D) 38 more stories than the building next door
   (E) 25 more stories than the building next door

50. A set of numbers includes all eleven of the integers from 10 to 20, inclusive. If a number is randomly selected from the set, what is the probability that the integer will be prime?

   (A) $\dfrac{4}{11}$

   (B) $\dfrac{2}{5}$

   (C) $\dfrac{5}{11}$

   (D) $\dfrac{1}{2}$

   (E) $\dfrac{3}{5}$

Number Concepts & Operations Practice –

Upper Level

1. Six boys are in line from shortest to tallest, each boy facing the back of the next taller boy. Ted is 4.07 feet tall. The heights of the other five boys are given below. How tall is the boy immediately in front of Ted?

   (A) 4 ft
   (B) 4.1 ft
   (C) 4.7 ft
   (D) 4.75 ft
   (E) 5 ft

2. The Summit School needs 150 pens. If pens are sold in boxes of 12, how many boxes of pens should The Summit School order?

   (A) 15
   (B) 14
   (C) 13
   (D) 12
   (E) 11

3. On average, Marin sells 100 pizza pies a day, and makes a profit of $2.75 on each pie. If her profits are cut to $2.50, how many more pizza pies will Marin have to sell in order to make the same daily profit as before?

   (A) 450
   (B) 50
   (C) 25
   (D) 15
   (E) 10

4. $\frac{1}{4} \times \frac{1}{3} \div \frac{1}{6} = ?$

    (A) $\frac{1}{2}$

    (B) $\frac{1}{3}$

    (C) $\frac{1}{4}$

    (D) $\frac{1}{6}$

    (E) $\frac{1}{12}$

5. In a class of n students, student must choose to take home economics or woodworking. For every student that chooses woodworking, twice as many choose home economics. Which of the following could be n?

    (A) 5
    (B) 10
    (C) 15
    (D) 20
    (E) 25

6. At 5 p.m., Chauncy realized that she had to return a book to the library by 5:30 p.m. If the library is 20 miles away, what must her average speed be in order to make it to the library by 5:30 p.m.?

    (A) 40 m.p.h.
    (B) 35 m.p.h.
    (C) 30 m.p.h.
    (D) 25 m.p.h.
    (E) 20 m.p.h.

7. Of the following, 50% of 3.75 is closest to

    (A) 3.00
    (B) 2.50
    (C) 2.25
    (D) 1.80
    (E) 1.50

8. Which of the following is closest to 20 percent of $7.90?

    (A) $1.40
    (B) $1.50
    (C) $1.60
    (D) $1.80
    (E) $2.00

9. A basketball player made 27 baskets in 12 games. How many baskets will the player make in 32 games if she continues to make baskets at the same rate?

    (A) 30
    (B) 45
    (C) 47
    (D) 72
    (E) 88

10. If $\dfrac{x}{100}$ is equal to 0.6, then x is equal to which of the following?

    (A) 0.006
    (B) 0.06
    (C) 6
    (D) 60
    (E) 600

11. List A contains all whole numbers between 9 and 13. List B contains all whole numbers between 11 and 14. Which of the following is a number in both lists?

    (A) 11
    (B) 11.5
    (C) 12
    (D) 12.5
    (E) 13

12. What is the best approximation of $2,097 \times 3,098$?

    (A) 600,000
    (B) 840,000
    (C) 6,500,000
    (D) 8,000,000
    (E) 8,400,000

SUMMIT
EDUCATIONAL
GROUP

13. No more than 7 clowns can get into a taxi at one time. If there are 39 clowns, how many taxis will they need?

(A) 1
(B) 5
(C) 6
(D) 7
(E) 14

14. 0.332×12 is closest to which of the following?

(A) $\frac{1}{3}$ of 10

(B) $\frac{1}{3}$ of 20

(C) $\frac{2}{3}$ of 10

(D) $\frac{2}{3}$ of 20

(E) $\frac{3}{10}$ of 10

15. Mr. Collins received apples from 7 of his students. If each of the students gave him the same number of apples, which of the following could be the total number of apples he received?

(A) 6
(B) 8
(C) 11
(D) 28
(E) 33

16. $50 - 4\frac{5}{9} =$

(A) $44\frac{4}{9}$

(B) $44\frac{7}{9}$

(C) $45\frac{2}{9}$

(D) $45\frac{4}{9}$

(E) $45\frac{8}{9}$

17. If the cafeteria is 200 feet long and the tables are 7 feet long, how many tables will fit end to end along the length of the cafeteria?

    (A) 28
    (B) 29
    (C) 30
    (D) 88
    (E) 89

18. $125 \times .101 =$

    (A) 1.2512
    (B) 1.2625
    (C) 12.625
    (D) 125.125
    (E) 126.25

19. Allen put 30% of the leaves in a pile in bags. If he bagged 300 leaves, how many leaves were originally in the pile?

    (A) 390
    (B) 700
    (C) 900
    (D) 1,000
    (E) 10,000

20. At 7 p.m., the water was 15 inches from the top of the sink. If the water rises at 1 inch per minute, how high is the water at 7:20 p.m.?

    (A) 14 inches from the top of the sink.
    (B) 10 inches from the top of the sink.
    (C) 5 inches from the top of the sink.
    (D) 1 inch from the top of the sink.
    (E) It has overflowed the sink.

21. Sally is thinking of the number 8.17. She will give a prize to the friend whose guess is closest to 8.17. The guesses are listed below. Which guess wins the prize?

    (A) 8
    (B) 9
    (C) 8.1
    (D) 8.2
    (E) 8.8

22. 35 percent of 19,889 is closest to which of the following?

    (A) 660
    (B) 6,100
    (C) 7,000
    (D) 8,500
    (E) 9,000

23. One pitcher of lemonade has 64 fluid ounces in it. Another pitcher has 52 fluid ounces in it. How many ounces must be poured from one pitcher to the other pitcher in order to make the amount of lemonade in each equal?

    (A) 6
    (B) 8
    (C) 10
    (D) 12
    (E) 22

24. With 6 weeks remaining before the fundraising deadline, Lisa has raised $57 more than Charlie has. For Charlie to raise as much money as Lisa, he must raise an average of at least how much more money per week than Lisa?

    (A) $9
    (B) $9.33
    (C) $9.50
    (D) $24
    (E) $84

25. Rounded to the nearest hundredth, what does $16 - 11\frac{7}{9}$ equal?

    (A) 0
    (B) 0.22
    (C) 0.89
    (D) 1.11
    (E) 4.22

26. Because of some great investments, Harry's income in 1998 was $8 million. This was 20 times his income in 1980. What was his income in 1980?

    (A) $4,000
    (B) $40,000
    (C) $80,000
    (D) $160,000
    (E) $400,000

27. Jack sold 9 cars, which was more than $\frac{1}{3}$ of the number of cars that were in his lot. The number of cars in his lot must have been

    (A) less than 3
    (B) greater than 3
    (C) equal to 12
    (D) less than 27
    (E) greater than 27

28. Which fraction is less than $\frac{1}{3}$?

    (A) $\frac{6}{15}$

    (B) $\frac{23}{66}$

    (C) $\frac{1000}{2999}$

    (D) $\frac{12}{39}$

    (E) $\frac{500}{900}$

29. All the following are equal to $\frac{2}{3}$ EXCEPT

   (A) $\frac{1}{4} \times \frac{16}{6}$

   (B) $\frac{4}{15} \times \frac{15}{6}$

   (C) $\frac{4}{6} \times \frac{100}{10}$

   (D) $\frac{2}{7} \times \frac{21}{9}$

   (E) $\frac{1}{8} \times \frac{16}{3}$

---

30. If 3 of every 10 people have red hair, how many redheads will there be in a group of 15,000 people?

   (A) 1,500
   (B) 3,000
   (C) 4,500
   (D) 5,000
   (E) 45,000

---

31. Jackie paid $2.40 in sales tax for her dress. If the sales tax was 6 percent, what was the price of the dress?

   (A) $2.40
   (B) $4.00
   (C) $14.40
   (D) $40.00
   (E) $42.00

---

32. 2,222.2 is how many times the value of 22.222?

   (A) $\frac{1}{100}$

   (B) $\frac{1}{10}$

   (C) 10
   (D) 100
   (E) 1,000

33. Bessie has 5 plots in her garden, and each plot has at least one flower. If no two plots have the same number of flowers, what is the smallest possible number of flowers in the garden?

    (A) 10
    (B) 15
    (C) 25
    (D) 50
    (E) 100

34. Patrick has 30 math problems to do from 6 p.m. to 9 p.m. By 6:20 p.m., he has finished 5 problems. If he continues to work at this rate, how much time will he have to spare when he has finished all 30 problems?

    (A) $\frac{1}{3}$ hr.
    (B) 1 hr.
    (C) $1\frac{2}{3}$ hrs.
    (D) 2 hrs.
    (E) He will not have enough time to finish before 9 p.m.

35. Matt's long distance call to France cost $4.95. The call was billed as follows: $1.25 for each of the first two minutes and $0.60 for every minute after that, except for the last minute, which is $1.25. How long did Matt's phone call last?

    (A) 3 minutes
    (B) 4 minutes
    (C) 5 minutes
    (D) 6 minutes
    (E) 7 minutes

36. What is the best estimate for 298 × 450?

    (A) 135,000
    (B) 150,000
    (C) 1,250,000
    (D) 1,350,000
    (E) 1,500,000

37. Of the 26 miles Jessie ran for the marathon, her fastest mile took 5 minutes and her slowest mile took 10 minutes. The number of hours it took Jessie to finish the marathon must have been between

(A) 2 and 5
(B) 3 and 5
(C) 4 and 6
(D) 5 and 6
(E) 5 and 7

38. On average, it takes Brian 1 hour and 45 minutes to finish each of his subjects for homework. If Brian starts his homework at 4 p.m. and has math, reading, social studies, and science to do, what time will it be when Brian is done with his homework?

(A) 9:20 p.m.
(B) 10:00 p.m.
(C) 10:40 p.m.
(D) 11:00 p.m.
(E) 11:20 p.m.

39. Another way of writing $\dfrac{9,000}{25} + \dfrac{500}{25} + \dfrac{40}{25}$ is

(A) $24.6\overline{)9,544}$

(B) $24.6\overline{)9,540.4}$

(C) $25\overline{)9,504}$

(D) $25\overline{)9,540}$

(E) $25\overline{)9,550}$

40. An elephant weighed 98 pounds at birth. After seven days, the elephant's weight had increased by 12%. Which of the following is closest to the elephant's weight at the end of the seventh day?

(A) 93 pounds
(B) 103 pounds
(C) 104 pounds
(D) 110 pounds
(E) 111 pounds

41. What is the value of $\dfrac{6^3}{3}-5(-4+9)$?

    (A) −13
    (B) 37
    (C) 47
    (D) 57
    (E) 97

42. If 3 cups of coffee cost $11.10, then, at that cost, what would be the price of 5 cups of coffee?

    (A) $13.50
    (B) $14.50
    (C) $15.50
    (D) $17.50
    (E) $18.50

43. Mrs. Kanter just won $750,000 in the lottery. She had to pay 40% in taxes. How much did she pay in taxes?

    (A) $25,250
    (B) $30,000
    (C) $250,250
    (D) $300,000
    (E) $325,500

44. Each of the 60 students in Mr. Collins's computer class own either a Macintosh or IBM computer. At the beginning of the year, half of the students owned Macintosh computers. Over the course of the year, 16 students traded their IBM computers for Macintosh computers. At the end of the year, how many more students owned Macintosh computers than owned IBM computers?

    (A) 14
    (B) 22
    (C) 32
    (D) 38
    (E) 46

45. 15 people in the office are planning to contribute $10 each to the boss's retirement party. Three of these people later decide not to contribute. How much more will each of the remaining people have to contribute so the office spends the same amount on the boss's retirement party?

    (A) $3.50
    (B) $3.25
    (C) $3.00
    (D) $2.75
    (E) $2.50

46. Louise was 4 feet $5\frac{1}{2}$ inches tall six years ago. She has grown $\frac{1}{4}$ of an inch per year since then. How tall is she now?

    (A) 4 feet and $5\frac{1}{4}$ inches

    (B) 4 feet and $5\frac{3}{4}$ inches

    (C) 4 feet and 6 inches

    (D) 4 feet and $6\frac{1}{2}$ inches

    (E) 4 feet and 7 inches

47. If the average of two numbers is 20, which of the following statements must be true?

    I.   If one of the two numbers is 11, the other number is less than 30.
    II. If a third number is added and the average jumps to 25, the third number is greater than 30.
    III. If each of the two numbers is reduced by 2, the average is reduced by 4.

    (A) I only
    (B) II only
    (C) III only
    (D) I and II only
    (E) I, II, and III

48. With $10, Leroy used to buy 10 tacos and still have $1.00 left over. But the price of tacos has gone up 10 cents per taco. With the price increase, how many tacos can Leroy afford to buy with $10 and still have $1.00 left over?

(A) 7
(B) 8
(C) 9
(D) 10
(E) 12

49. If $2A$ is an odd integer, which of the following must be true?

I. A is not an integer.
II. $3A$ is also an odd integer.
III. $3A + 1$ is also an odd integer.

(A) I only
(B) III only
(C) I and III only
(D) I and II only
(E) I, II, and III

50. x and y are prime numbers with a product of 91. What is the difference between x and y?

(A) 5
(B) 6
(C) 7
(D) 8
(E) 9

SUMMIT
EDUCATIONAL
GROUP

Algebra

❑ Absolute Value   146

❑ Scientific Notation   148

❑ Exponents   150

❑ Roots   154

❑ Expressions   158

❑ Equations   162

❑ Inequalities   166

❑ Simultaneous Equations   170

❑ Translating   174

❑ Functions   178

❑ SSAT Functions   180

❑ Quadratic Equations   184

Algebra

❏ Algebra is a form of math that uses numbers, symbols and letters to solve problems.

❏ In this chapter, you will:

- learn how to solve algebraic equations.

- learn to translate and solve word problems.

- learn how to attack "SSAT function" problems.

- learn how to solve inequalities.

Vocabulary

❑ **Terms** are the parts of an expression and are separated by + and − signs.

❑ **Variables** are letters (and sometimes symbols) used to represent numbers in algebraic expressions and equations.

❑ A **constant** is a fixed number. Constants are terms that do not contain variables.

❑ An **algebraic expression** is a phrase that contains one or more terms and does not contain an equal sign. An expression can include constants, variables, and operating symbols (such as addition signs and exponents).

❑ An **equation** is a statement that two expressions are equal.

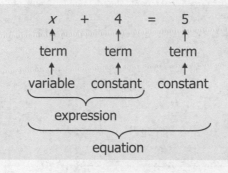

Absolute Value

The absolute value of a number is the distance between the number and zero on the number line. Think of the absolute value of a number as the "positive value" of that number.

Most absolute value questions can be solved with basic algebra skills. When solving absolute value problems, be very careful with positive and negative signs.

❑ To simplify an expression within an absolute value sign, simplify just as you would simplify an expression in parentheses. Then take the absolute value of the result.

$|7(-3) + 4(5)| = $ _____

$|5 - 3| - |6 - 9| = $ _____

❑ Taking the absolute value of a number always results in a positive number.

$|2| = ?$

$|-2| = ?$

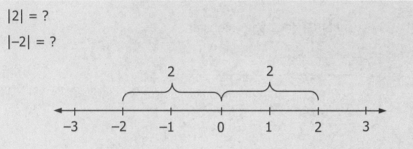

The distance between 2 and 0 is 2. The distance between −2 and 0 is also 2.

So, $|2| = 2$ and $|-2| = 2$.

TRY IT OUT

1. $|-7| =$

2. $|10| =$

3. $|3(-2)| =$

4. $|1 + (-7)| =$

5. $-|-4| =$

6. $-2|2 - 3| =$

Use the number line below to answer questions 7–10:

$$A \quad B \quad -1 \quad 0 \quad C \quad D \quad E$$

7. $|A| =$

8. $|C| =$

9. $|B - D| =$

10. $|A - E| =$

PUT IT TOGETHER

1. $-4|-8 + 1| = ?$

    (A) -33
    (B) -28
    (C) -3
    (D) 28
    (E) 33

---

2. If $|x| = x + 6$, then $x = ?$

    (A) -12
    (B) -6
    (C) -3
    (D) 3
    (E) 6

---

3. If $a > b$, then $|b - a|$ is equivalent to which of the following?

    (A) $a + b$
    (B) $a - b$
    (C) $b - a$
    (D) $-(a + b)$
    (E) $-(a - b)$

Scientific Notation

❑ In "scientific notation," a number is written so that the largest digit is in the units place, and it is multiplied by a power of 10.

$$3{,}642{,}000{,}000{,}000 = 3.642 \times 10^{12} \qquad\qquad 0.00000000146 = 1.46 \times 10^{-9}$$

❑ To convert a number written in scientific notation to regular decimal format, simply move the decimal point according to the exponent on the 10.

If the exponent is positive, move the decimal to the right by that many places. If the exponent is negative, move the decimal to the left by that many places.

Write 0.000000000000678 in scientific notation:

Write 8.63×10^6 in decimal format:

The minimum distance from Earth to Saturn is about 8.0×10^8 miles. If light travels at a speed of about 2.0×10^5 miles per second, how long will it take light to travel from Earth to Saturn?

Use this formula: speed × time = distance

Rewrite formula with given values: _____

Set equation equal to time: _____

Simplify: _____

How long will it take light to travel from Earth to Saturn? _____

PUT IT TOGETHER

1. Which of the following numbers is greatest in value?

    (A) 1.4×10^8
    (B) 140×10^4
    (C) 0.14×10^7
    (D) 140,000
    (E) 0.0014×10^9

---

2. A person takes in 1.25×10^{22} molecules of air with each breath. 20% of the air is comprised of oxygen molecules. If only 5% of the oxygen molecules are absorbed, how many oxygen molecules are absorbed in one breath?

    (A) 50,000,000,000,000,000,000,000
    (B) 12,500,000,000,000,000,000,000
    (C) 500,000,000,000,000,000,000
    (D) 125,000,000,000,000,000,000
    (E) 1,250,000,000,000,000,000

Exponents

❑ An exponent tells you how many times to multiply a number by itself.

$$4^3 = 4 \times 4 \times 4 \qquad 2x^5 = 2 \cdot x \cdot x \cdot x \cdot x \cdot x \qquad (7y)^3 = 7y \cdot 7y \cdot 7y$$

❑ Know the following properties of exponents:

Any base raised to an exponent of 0 equals 1.

$$3^0 = 1 \qquad\qquad\qquad 21^0 = \underline{\hspace{1.5cm}}$$

A base with an exponent of 1 is equal to the base.

$$7^1 = 7 \qquad\qquad\qquad 100^1 = \underline{\hspace{1.5cm}}$$

A number greater than 1 raised to a power greater than 1 becomes larger.

$$2^4 = 16 \qquad\qquad\qquad 3^3 = \underline{\hspace{1.5cm}}$$

When a fraction is raised to an exponent, apply the exponent to both the numerator and the denominator.

$$\left(\frac{1}{2}\right)^2 = \frac{1}{4} \qquad\qquad\qquad \left(\frac{2}{3}\right)^2 = \underline{\hspace{1.5cm}}$$

A positive fraction less than 1 raised to a power greater than 1 becomes smaller.

$$\left(\frac{1}{4}\right)^2 = \frac{1}{16} \qquad\qquad\qquad \left(\frac{1}{3}\right)^4 = \underline{\hspace{1.5cm}}$$

A negative number raised to an even power becomes positive.

$$(-1)^4 = 1 \qquad\qquad\qquad (-4)^2 = \underline{\hspace{1.5cm}}$$

A negative number raised to an odd power remains negative.

$$(-1)^5 = -1 \qquad\qquad\qquad (-2)^3 = \underline{\hspace{1.5cm}}$$

TRY IT OUT

Simplify:

1. $2^0 =$

2. $2^1 =$

3. $2^3 =$

4. $(-2)^2 =$

5. $(-2)^3 =$

6. $(-2)^4 =$

7. $(-1)^{100} =$

8. $(-1)^{101} =$

9. $\left(\dfrac{1}{3}\right)^2 =$

10. $\left(\dfrac{2}{3}\right)^3 =$

Solve:

11. If $x^2 = 9$, then $x =$

12. If $x^3 = 64$, then $x =$

13. If $x^3 = -8$, then $x =$

14. If $x^5 = -1$, then $x =$

15. If $x^2 = \dfrac{1}{100}$, then $x =$

16. If $5^x = 125$, then $x =$

PUT IT TOGETHER

1. Which of the following is true?

    (A) $2^2 = 4^4$
    (B) $2^2 > 4^4$
    (C) $2^4 < 4^2$
    (D) $2^4 = 4^2$
    (E) $2^4 > 4^2$

---

2. If $5^{x-1} = 1$, which of the following is the value of x?

    (A) -2
    (B) -1
    (C) 0
    (D) 1
    (E) 2

Multiplying and Dividing Numbers with Exponents

❑ To multiply two numbers with the same base, add the exponents.

$x^a \cdot x^b = x^{a+b}$

$m^2 \times m^4$ ⇨ $(m \cdot m) \cdot (m \cdot m \cdot m \cdot m)$ ⇨ $m \cdot m \cdot m \cdot m \cdot m \cdot m$ ⇨ m^6

$2^2 \times 2^5 = 2^{2+5} = 2^7$ $t \times t^4 =$ _____

Note: $3^2 + 3^4$ does not equal 3^6

❑ To divide two numbers with the same base, subtract the exponents.

$x^a \div x^b = x^{a-b}$

$m^5 \div m^2$ ⇨ $\dfrac{m \cdot m \cdot m \cdot m \cdot m}{m \cdot m}$ ⇨ $\dfrac{m \cdot m \cdot m}{1}$ ⇨ m^3

$\dfrac{3^5}{3^2} = 3^{5-2} = 3^3$ $\dfrac{b^6}{b^5} =$ _____

Note: $x^5 - x^2$ does not equal x^3

❑ To raise a power to a power, multiply the exponents.

$\left(x^a\right)^b = x^{ab}$

$\left(m^2\right)^3$ ⇨ $\left(m^2\right) \cdot \left(m^2\right) \cdot \left(m^2\right)$ ⇨ $m \cdot m \cdot m \cdot m \cdot m \cdot m$ ⇨ m^6

$\left(2^3\right)^7 =$ _____ $\left(d^3\right)^5 =$ _____

❑ Pay special attention to parentheses when dealing with exponents. Each "piece" inside the parentheses must be raised to the exponent.

$\left(5x^2\right)^3$ ⇨ $(5)^3 \cdot \left(x^2\right)^3$ ⇨ $125 \cdot x^6$ ⇨ $125x^6$

TRY IT OUT

Simplify:

1. $2^2 \times 2^3 =$

2. $x^4 \cdot x^3 =$

3. $\dfrac{7^3}{7^2} =$

4. $\dfrac{x^{12}}{x^2} =$

5. $\left(6^3\right)^2 =$

6. $\left(x^{11}\right)^4 =$

7. $\left(4x^3\right)^7 =$

PUT IT TOGETHER

1. $\left(3x^2y\right)^3 =$

    (A) $3x^2y^3$
    (B) $3x^5y^3$
    (C) $9x^6y^3$
    (D) $27x^5y^3$
    (E) $27x^6y^3$

    _____

2. If $\left(x^{t+1}\right)^3 = x^9$, what is the value of t?

    (A) 2
    (B) 3
    (C) 4
    (D) 5
    (E) 6

Roots

❑ A **square root** (also known as a **radical**) is an exponent of 2 in reverse.

A number's square root is the number which, when multiplied by itself, gives you the original number.

$\sqrt{81} = 9$ because $9 \times 9 = 81$.

$\sqrt{x} \cdot \sqrt{x} = x$ because $\sqrt{x^2} = x$.

❑ To simplify a square root, factor out any square factors. It helps to separate the number in the radical into the product of multiple radicals.

$\sqrt{50}$ ⇨ $\sqrt{25 \times 2}$ ⇨ $\sqrt{25} \times \sqrt{2}$ ⇨ $5\sqrt{2}$

❑ A **cubic root** is an exponent of 3 in reverse.

$\sqrt[3]{8} = 2$ because $2 \times 2 \times 2 = 8$.

$\sqrt[3]{-27} = -3$ because $-3 \times -3 \times -3 = -27$.

❑ You can save time on roots problems by memorizing common roots.

$\sqrt{4} = $ _____ $\sqrt{16} = $ _____

$\sqrt{1} = $ _____ $\sqrt{121} = $ _____

$\sqrt{100} = $ _____ $\sqrt{81} = $ _____

$\sqrt{9} = $ _____ $\sqrt{64} = $ _____

$\sqrt{25} = $ _____ $\sqrt{49} = $ _____

$\sqrt{36} = $ _____ $\sqrt{144} = $ _____

❑ Roots can be expressed as fractional exponents.

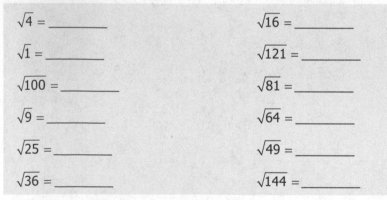

$400^{\frac{1}{2}} = \sqrt{400} = $ _____ $64^{\frac{3}{2}} = 64^{\left(\frac{1}{2} \times 3\right)} = \left(\sqrt{64}\right)^3 = $ _____

$125^{\frac{1}{3}} = \sqrt[3]{125} = $ _____ $27^{\frac{2}{3}} = 27^{\left(\frac{1}{3} \times 2\right)} = \left(\sqrt[3]{27}\right)^2 = $ _____

TRY IT OUT

Simplify the following radicals:

1. $\sqrt{16}$

2. $\sqrt{49}$

3. $\sqrt{\dfrac{1}{9}}$

4. $\sqrt{\dfrac{4}{9}}$

5. $\sqrt{x^2}$

6. $\sqrt{x^4}$

7. $\sqrt{4x^{10}}$

8. $\sqrt[3]{1000}$

9. $\sqrt[3]{64}$

10. $\sqrt[3]{-1}$

11. $\sqrt[3]{-125}$

12. $\sqrt[3]{\dfrac{1}{8}}$

13. $\sqrt{8}$

14. $\sqrt{12}$

15. $\sqrt{80}$

16. $\sqrt{32}$

PUT IT TOGETHER

1. $\sqrt{41}$ is closest to what number?

    (A) 3
    (B) 4
    (C) 5
    (D) 6
    (E) 7

---

2. $\sqrt{3} \times \sqrt{3} =$

    (A) 1
    (B) $\sqrt{6}$
    (C) 3
    (D) 9
    (E) 30

Checkpoint Review

1. $|2 \times (-6) - (-3 \times 7)| =$

   (A) 54
   (B) 33
   (C) 30
   (D) 18
   (E) 9

2. What is $\dfrac{1}{50,000}$ expressed in scientific notation?

   (A) 5.0×10^{-4}
   (B) 2.0×10^{-4}
   (C) 5.0×10^{-5}
   (D) 2.0×10^{-5}
   (E) 5.0×10^{-6}

3. If $|x| = x + 4$, then $x = ?$

   (A) -8
   (B) -4
   (C) -2
   (D) 2
   (E) 4

4. The minimum distance between Earth and Mars is 5.46×10^7 kilometers. The minimum distance between Earth and Jupiter is 5.88×10^8 kilometers. How much farther, in kilometers, is the minimum distance from Earth to Jupiter than from Earth to Mars?

   (A) 5.334×10^8
   (B) 4.872×10^8
   (C) 5.334×10^7
   (D) 4.872×10^7
   (E) 4.2×10^6

Checkpoint Review

5. Which of the following expressions is equivalent to $\sqrt[4]{x^{10}}$?

   (A) x^{-6}

   (B) x^6

   (C) x^3

   (D) $x^{\frac{5}{2}}$

   (E) $x^{\frac{2}{5}}$

---

6. Which of the following is equivalent to $\sqrt{27} - \sqrt{12}$?

   (A) 1

   (B) $\sqrt{3}$

   (C) 3

   (D) $2\sqrt{3}$

   (E) $4\sqrt{3}$

---

7. Which expression is equivalent to $\sqrt{80x^{16}}$?

   (A) $4x^4\sqrt{5}$

   (B) $4x^8\sqrt{5}$

   (C) $16x^4\sqrt{5}$

   (D) $16x^8\sqrt{5}$

   (E) $40x^8$

---

8. What is the difference between the cube roots of 27 and 216?

   (A) 3

   (B) 9

   (C) 18

   (D) 63

   (E) 189

Algebraic Expressions

An algebraic expression is a phrase that contains one or more terms and does not contain an equal sign. An expression can include constants, variables, and operating symbols (such as addition signs and exponents).

Most expressions questions are relatively simple and straightforward. However, they may require several steps, so make sure you work carefully and follow the Order of Operations.

❑ **Simplifying** an algebraic expression is often the first step in solving an algebraic equation.

   To simplify an algebraic expression, combine similar terms.

   $4 + x + 5 - 3x - 9$ ⇨ $(4 + 5 - 9) + (x - 3x)$ ⇨ $0 + (-2x) = -2x$

❑ Use the **distributive property** to multiply a single term by an expression inside parentheses.

   $2(x + y)$ ⇨ $2(x + y)$ ⇨ $(2x) + (2y)$ ⇨ $2x + 2y$

   Be careful when distributing a negative number. You must carry the negative sign through the entire distribution.

   $-6(2x - 4)$ ⇨ $(-6 \times 2x) - (-6 \times 4)$ ⇨ $(-12x) - (-24)$ ⇨ $-12x + 24$

❑ **F.O.I.L.** – When multiplying two binomials, each term must be multiplied by each term in the other binomial. Use the FOIL method: multiply the first terms, outside terms, inside terms, and last terms.

   $(3y + 6)(y - 5) = $ _____

❑ Algebraic expressions can be used to express situations in math terms.

   Levi found 3 more bottle caps for his collection.   ⇨ $C + 3$

   The amount Vanessa paid for 2 shirts and 4 dresses.   ⇨ $2S + 4D$

   The price of the tickets increased by 10%.   ⇨ $T + (10\% \times T)$

   Whitney spent a fourth of her savings.   ⇨ $S - (S \div 4)$

TRY IT OUT

Simplify the following expressions:

1. $13 + 4 + x + 2x$

2. $4 - x + 8 + 2x$

3. $1 + 2x + 8 - x - 9 - 5x$

4. $x^2 + 4 + 2x^2 - 1$

5. $2x^2 - x + 7 - 5x^2 + 5 + 6x$

6. $(2x + 1) + (x + 9)$

7. $(7 + 4x) - (6 + 3x)$

8. $(x - 3) + (4 + 2x)$

9. $(4 - 8x) - (6x - 3)$

10. $2(x + 3)$

11. $4(2x + 7)$

12. $-1(3 + 4x)$

13. $-3(x + 6)$

14. $-7(6 - 5x)$

15. $x(x + 1)$

16. $2x(x - 6)$

17. $-5x(x + 4)$

18. $-2x(-9 - 4x)$

19. $2(x + 3) + 4(5x - 1)$

20. $5x(x - 1) - 7(x + 2)$

SUMMIT
EDUCATIONAL
GROUP

PUT IT TOGETHER

1. Which of the following gives the number of cents in x
    pennies, y dimes, and 2 dollars?

    (A) $200 + x + 10y$
    (B) $200 + 1 + 10$
    (C) $2 + x + 10y$
    (D) $2 + 1 + 10y$
    (E) $2 + 1 + 10$

2. Marion bought half a dozen muffins that cost $1.50 each.
    Which of the following is a way to find how much she
    spent in <u>dollars</u>?

    (A) $6 \times 1\frac{1}{2}$

    (B) 6×150

    (C) $6 \times \dfrac{1.50}{2}$

    (D) $6 \times \dfrac{150}{2}$

    (E) $\dfrac{1}{6} \times 150$

3. If N is a whole number, then which of the following
    numbers can be written as $5N + 3$?

    (A) 15
    (B) 35
    (C) 37
    (D) 48
    (E) 50

4. $\frac{1}{2}x + 4$

    If x is a whole number, the expression shown above could represent which of the following?

    I.   The number of hours William does homework in a day if he works for half an hour four times

    II. The number of miles it takes to drive halfway to a destination that is more than four miles away

    III. The number of people left in a club if half the members leave and then four more members join

    (A) I only
    (B) III only
    (C) I and II only
    (D) I and III only
    (E) I, II, and III

    _____

5. In the expression $\frac{x}{yz}$, if x, y, and z are each doubled, then the original expression is

    (A) multiplied by 2
    (B) multiplied by 4
    (C) divided by 2
    (D) divided by 4
    (E) left unchanged

    _____

6. Which expression is equivalent to $(2x^2 + 3x - 2)(x + 3)$?

    (A) $8x^3 + 12x^2 - 8x$
    (B) $2x^3 + 9x^2 + 7x - 6$
    (C) $2x^3 - 3x^2 - 11x + 6$
    (D) $2x^3 - 3x^2 - 11x - 8$
    (E) $8x^2 + 12x - 8$

Algebraic Equations

❏ To solve an equation, get the variable by itself on one side of the equal sign.

Keep the equation balanced. If you do something to one side, such as add a number or divide by a number, you must do the same to the other side.

> Solve for x: $5x + 10 = 30$
>
> We will try to get the x alone on the left side of the equal sign.
>
> Step 1: Subtract 10 from both sides.   Step 2: Divide both sides by 5.
>
> $5x + 10 = 30$
>
> $-10 \quad -10$ $5x = 20 \implies \dfrac{5x}{5} = \dfrac{20}{5} \implies x = 4$
>
> $5x \quad\quad = 20$

❏ When multiplying or dividing by a negative number, **pay close attention to signs**.
Remember: Negative × Negative = Positive, and Negative × Positive = Negative

> $-2x - 8 = 14 \implies -2x - 8 = 14 \implies \dfrac{(-2x-8)}{-2} = \dfrac{(14)}{-2} \implies$ _____

❏ **To solve an equation with a fraction**, first get rid of the fraction by multiplying both sides of the equation by the denominator. Then solve the equation using basic strategies.

> $\dfrac{x}{2} + 1 = 4 \implies \dfrac{x}{2} + 1 = 4 \implies \left(\dfrac{x}{2} + 1\right) \times 2 = (4) \times 2 \implies x + 2 = 8 \implies x = 6$

> If $\dfrac{3x}{4} + \dfrac{1}{2} = 5$, what is the value of x? _____

❏ **To solve an equation with a square root**, first get rid of the radical sign by isolating the radical on one side of the equation and then squaring both sides. Then solve the equation using basic strategies.

> If $1 + \sqrt{x} = 8$, what is the value of x?
>
> Get the radical alone on one side of the equation: _____
>
> Square each side of the equation to get rid of radical sign: _____

TRY IT OUT

For each equation, find the value of the variable:

1. $R - 1 = 10$

2. $n + 5 = 10$

3. $(25{,}000) \times 0 = N$

4. $x + 1 = 1{,}001$

5. $\Delta + 100 = 150$

6. $100 \times N = 100$

7. $4 + x + 4 = 28$

8. $S - 20 = 105$

9. $36 - T = 26$

10. $2N + N = 60$

11. 50% of y equals 30.

12. $2x + 3 = 27$

13. $4x - 2 = 14$

14. $\dfrac{1}{2}n = 50$

15. $\dfrac{1}{3}n + 4 = 10$

16. $\dfrac{2x}{3} - 1 = \dfrac{13}{2}$

17. $\sqrt{x} = 4$

18. $\sqrt{x + 2} = 10$

19. $2 - \sqrt{3x + 4} = 2 - x$

20. $\sqrt[4]{2x} = 2$

SUMMIT
EDUCATIONAL
GROUP

PUT IT TOGETHER

1. If $16 \times N = 16$, then $16 + N =$

   (A) 1
   (B) 15
   (C) 16
   (D) 17
   (E) 32

2. Which is true when $x = 9$?

   (A) $2x + 1 = 20$
   (B) $14 = 2x - 5$
   (C) $x + 2 \times 4 = 44$
   (D) $5(x - 4) = 25$
   (E) $44 = 5 + 3x$

3. If $x + 10 = y$, then $x + 17 =$

   (A) $y - 7$
   (B) $y - 3$
   (C) $y + 3$
   (D) $y + 7$
   (E) $y + 10$

4. If $2 + x + y = 18$, what is the value of $x + y$?

   (A) 7
   (B) 8
   (C) 9
   (D) 11
   (E) 16

5. If $m + 2n = 2m + n$, which of the following must be true?

   (A) $m = n$
   (B) $m = 2n$
   (C) $2m = n$
   (D) $3m = n$
   (E) $3 = mn$

6. If $2x - y = 7$ and $4 + 3y = 19$, then $x - y = ?$

(A) −3
(B) −2
(C) 1
(D) 3
(E) 8

7. What is the value of x if $13x + (5 - 9x) = 2(9 - 2x)$?

(A) $2\dfrac{7}{8}$

(B) 2

(C) $1\dfrac{3}{4}$

(D) $1\dfrac{5}{8}$

(E) $\dfrac{1}{2}$

8. If $\sqrt{2x + 5} = x + 1$, what is the value of x?

(A) −1
(B) 0
(C) $\dfrac{1}{2}$
(D) 1
(E) 2

Inequalities

❑ An inequality contains one of the following symbols:

> greater than

< less than

≥ greater than or equal to

≤ less than or equal to

❑ The solution to an inequality can be a range of numbers.

> *N* is a number between 6 and 11. What are the possible values of *N*?

> *N* is an odd number greater than 5 but less than 20. What are the possible values of *N*?

❑ Inequalities can be solved just like equations, with one important difference: if you multiply or divide both sides by a negative number, you must switch the direction of the inequality sign.

$2x + 4 < 10$ ⇨ $2x + 4 < 10$ ⇨ $2x < 6$ ⇨ $2x < 6$ ⇨ $x < 3$
                          $-4 \quad -4$ $\div 2 \quad \div 2$

$-2x + 4 < 10$ ⇨ $-2x + 4 < 10$ ⇨ $-2x < 6$ ⇨ $-2x < 6$ ⇨ $x > 3$
                            $-4 \quad -4$ $\div -2 \quad \div -2$ ↺

TRY IT OUT

Write the set of numbers that expresses the possible values for each of the following variables.

1. N is a whole number between 2 and 5.

2. T is a positive odd number less than 9.

3. X is a negative integer greater than –3.

Write the inequality that expresses the range of possible values for each of the following variables.

4. $n + 2 > 6$

5. $x - 5 \le 13$

6. $3x + 2 < 8$

7. $4s - 3 \ge 3$

8. $-x + 6 > 10$

9. $-2r + 1 < 7$

10. $-3m - 1 > -10$

PUT IT TOGETHER

1.   If $5 < N < 10$, and N is a multiple of 4, then $N =$

(A) -4
(B) 0
(C) 4
(D) 8
(E) 12

---

2.   If half a certain number is greater than 21, then the number can be which of the following?

(A) 10
(B) 11
(C) 22
(D) 42
(E) 84

---

3.   If the value of $\frac{1}{3} + N < 1$, then N could be each of the following EXCEPT

(A) $\frac{1}{3}$

(B) $\frac{1}{2}$

(C) $\frac{2}{3}$

(D) $\frac{3}{5}$

(E) $\frac{5}{8}$

4. If $x < 3$, then $4x + 11$ could be

    (A) 41
    (B) 27
    (C) 24
    (D) 23
    (E) 0

___

5. If $3(M + N) < 0$, then which of the following must be true?

    (A) $M > N$
    (B) $M < N$
    (C) $M - N > 0$
    (D) $M + N < 0$
    (E) $N - M < 0$

___

6. Which of the following represents the solution to the inequality $-(3x - 6) > 3(-3 - 2x)$ on the number line?

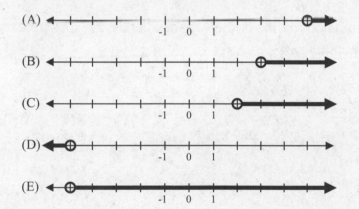

___

Simultaneous Equations

To solve simultaneous equations (also called **systems of equations**), you must know the elimination and substitution methods, as well as how to set up equations from word problems.

❑ **Elimination Method** – Add or subtract equations to cancel one of the variables and solve for the other. You may have to multiply an equation by some number to eliminate a variable before the equations are added or subtracted.

> If $2x + y = 16$ and $x - 2y = 3$, what is the value of x?
>
> Stack the equations: $2x + y = 16$
> $x - 2y = 3$
>
> What do you need to multiply the top equation by to make the y disappear when you
>
> add the two equations? _____
>
> Rewrite the equations and add them. Solve for x.

❑ **Substitution Method** – Solve one equation for one of the variables, and then substitute that value for that variable in the other equation.

> If $2x + y = 3$ and $-x - 3y = 6$, what is the value of x?
>
> Solve the equation $2x + y = 3$ for y: _____
>
> Substitute that value for y in the other equation: $-x - 3(\underline{\hspace{2cm}}) = 6$
>
> Solve for x.

❑ **Simultaneous Equations in Word Problems** – Word problems that require you to define two variables are often simultaneous equation questions. Learn to recognize them and translate to set up the equations.

> 1000 tickets were sold to the Seaport Aquarium's Dolphin Show. Adult tickets cost $10, children's tickets cost $2, and a total of $5200 was collected. How many adult tickets were sold?
>
> What are your two variables? Define them.
>
> A = number of Adult tickets sold
>
>
>
> $C =$ _____
>
> Write an equation for the total number of tickets: $A + C = 1000$
>
> Write an equation for the total cost of the tickets: _____
>
> Solve the simultaneous equations for A.

PUT IT TOGETHER

1. $2x - y = 5$
    $x + 3y = 6$

    For the system of equations shown above, what is the value of y?

    (A) 1
    (B) 2
    (C) 3
    (D) 4
    (E) 5

___

2. A guitar and case sold for a regular price of $200 total. During a sale, the guitar was sold for half its regular price, and the total price for the guitar and case was $120. What was the price of the case?

    (A) $20
    (B) $40
    (C) $50
    (D) $60
    (E) $80

___

3. Three times Bradley's age decreased by three times Isaac's age equals 12. Bradley's age increased by twice Isaac's age equals 115. What is Bradley's age?

    (A) 34
    (B) 36
    (C) 37
    (D) 41
    (E) 43

Checkpoint Review

1. If $3 - ax \geq 27$, what value of a will result in the solution $x \geq 6$?

    (A) -8
    (B) -5
    (C) -4
    (D) 4
    (E) 5

2. If $x^2 = 225$, what is the value of $(x - 1)^2$?

    (A) 16
    (B) 196
    (C) 226
    (D) 256
    (E) 676

3.

x	y
-3	25
-1	13
1	1
3	-11

Which equation describes the function displayed in the table shown above?

    (A) $y = -6x - 7$
    (B) $y = -6x + 7$
    (C) $y = 6x - 7$
    (D) $y = 6x + 7$
    (E) $y = 7x - 6$

4. The price for entrance tickets to an aquarium is $83 for 2 adults and 3 children. For 3 adults and 1 child, the price is $79. What is the price of an entrance ticket for 1 adult?

    (A) $12
    (B) $13
    (C) $22
    (D) $23
    (E) $33

Checkpoint Review

5. Which of the following expressions is equivalent to
    $\left(x+\dfrac{2}{3}\right)-\dfrac{2x-5}{3}$?

    (A) $\dfrac{x+7}{3}$

    (B) $\dfrac{x}{3}-1$

    (C) $\dfrac{x}{3}+1$

    (D) $-\dfrac{x}{3}-1$

    (E) $-\dfrac{x}{3}+1$

---

6. The volume of a sphere is $V=\dfrac{4}{3}\pi r^3$. Which of the
    following equations is this equation solved for r?

    (A) $r=\sqrt[3]{\dfrac{3V}{4\pi}}$

    (B) $r=\dfrac{\sqrt[3]{3V}}{4\pi}$

    (C) $r=\dfrac{3\sqrt[3]{V}}{4\pi}$

    (D) $r=\left(\dfrac{3}{4}\right)\sqrt[3]{\dfrac{V}{\pi}}$

    (E) $r=\left(\dfrac{V}{\pi}\right)\sqrt[3]{\dfrac{3}{4}}$

Translating

❑ Transforming words into mathematical equations is the first step in solving many SSAT problems. It is especially helpful in solving word problems.

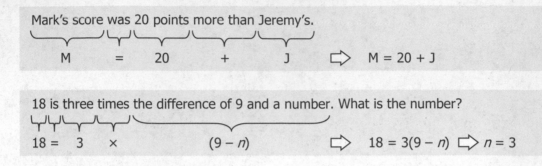

Mark's score was 20 points more than Jeremy's.

M   =   20   +   J   ⟹   M = 20 + J

18 is three times the difference of 9 and a number. What is the number?

18 =   3   ×   (9 − n)   ⟹   18 = 3(9 − n)   ⟹   n = 3

❑ After reading the question, state in your own words what the problem is asking you to find. Break the problem into its parts and make certain you understand each of them. Translate the parts into "math language," and use the math equations you have set up to get the answer.

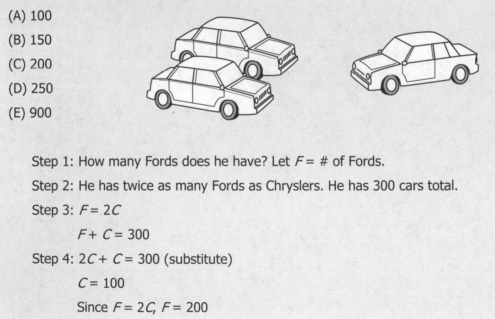

A car dealer has twice as many Fords as Chryslers. He has 300 cars total. How many Fords does he have?

(A) 100

(B) 150

(C) 200

(D) 250

(E) 900

Step 1: How many Fords does he have? Let F = # of Fords.

Step 2: He has twice as many Fords as Chryslers. He has 300 cars total.

Step 3: $F = 2C$

$F + C = 300$

Step 4: $2C + C = 300$ (substitute)

$C = 100$

Since $F = 2C$, $F = 200$

TRY IT OUT

Change the following to mathematical equations, and solve for variables when possible:

1. 50% of 24 is x.

2. 6 fewer than y is 17.

3. 1/2 of 28 is what?

4. u more than 9 is a.

5. 1 increased by z equals what?

6. The sum of u, v, and w is 9.

7. The product of 7 and 4 is y.

8. −5 is the average of a, b, and c.

9. Sam is 2 years younger than Fred.

10. Twice N increased by 1 is 11.

Try the following word problems:

11. Five less than seven times a certain number is 58. Find the number.

12. Tommy has six times as many apples as Bobby. Bobby has 7 more apples than Alice. If Alice has 2 apples, how many apples does Tommy have?

13. Suzy has 3 times as many marbles as Marty. Marty has 4 marbles less than Joey. If together they have 34 marbles, how many marbles does Joey have?

14. The length of a rectangle is 2 more than the width. If the perimeter of the rectangle is 48, what is the width of the rectangle?

15. The sum of 2 numbers is 18 and their difference is 8. What is the larger of the two numbers?

PUT IT TOGETHER

1. Last year, Mark read t more books than Rob did. If Rob read 6 books last year, how many books did Mark read last year?

    (A) 6
    (B) $6 + t$
    (C) $6 - t$
    (D) $6 \times t$
    (E) It cannot be determined from the information given.

    _____

2. There are x types of pastries available in a bakery and 5 of them contain nuts. In terms of x how many of the pastries in the bakery do not contain nuts?

    (A) $5x$
    (B) $5 + x$
    (C) $5 - x$
    (D) $x - 5$
    (E) $x \div 5$

    _____

3. Andy had N tokens more than twice as many tokens as Drew has. If Drew has 18 tokens, how many tokens does Andy have?

    (A) $18 + 2N$
    (B) $36 + 2N$
    (C) $36 - 2N$
    (D) $36 + N$
    (E) $36 - N$

    _____

4. Xavier has three times as many cards as Anna has. If Anna has N cards, which of the following expressions represents the total number of cards they have together?

    (A) $N + N$
    (B) $3N$
    (C) $3 + N$
    (D) $3N + N$
    (E) $3 \times (N + N)$

5. Ellis has collected x action figures. Max has 6 fewer action figures than Ellis has. Which of the following expressions best represents the number of action figures Max will have if he buys 4 figures from Ellis?

(A) $x - 10$
(B) $x - 6$
(C) $x - 2$
(D) $x + 6$
(E) $x + 10$

---

6. If the average of x and y is 100 and $x < y$, which of the following must be true?

(A) $x = 200 - y$
(B) $x = 100 + y$
(C) $x = y - 100$
(D) $x + y = 100$
(E) $x - y = 100$

---

7. A biologist determines that the population of a species of gecko y years after 2001 is represented by the expression $6{,}100(0.92)^y$. According to the biologist, by what percent does the gecko population change each year?

(A) 8%
(B) 92%
(C) 98%
(D) 102%
(E) 108%

Functions

❑ A function is an "instruction" or "process" that, for any value of x you put in, will give you a single value of y (or $f(x)$) as a result. You can think of a function as a machine that takes inputs and converts them to outputs. You input a value for x, and the machine puts out a value for $f(x)$.

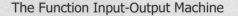

The Function Input-Output Machine

Input a value for x:

$x = 9$

$f(x) = x^2$

Out comes a value for $f(x)$:

$f(9) = 9^2 = 81$

Think of the function $f(x) = x^2$ as a machine that always does the same thing. This machine will take any value and square it.

A function equation is like a machine's manual that explains what the function does with any input value.

❑ To **evaluate a function**, $f(x)$, for a particular value of x, simply substitute that value everywhere you see an x.

Consider the following function: $f(x) = 3x - 2$

$f(5) = 3(5) - 2 = 13$

$f(1) =$ _____

$f(-t) =$ _____

If $f(a) = 49$, what is the value of a ? _____

TRY IT OUT

1. If $f(x) = 2x - 1$, then $f(2) =$

2. If $f(x) = x^2 + 3$, and $x = 5$, then $f(x) =$

3. If $f(x) = x + 7$, and $f(a) = 3$, then $a =$

PUT IT TOGETHER

1. What is the value of $f(-5)$ for the function
    $f(x) = 2x^3 - 4x^2 - 16$?

    (A) 134
    (B) –134
    (C) –166
    (D) –334
    (E) –366

---

2. For the function $f(x) = (x - 1)^2 + 2$, what is the average
    rate of change over the interval $x = 3$ to $x = 7$?

    (A) 6.4
    (B) 7.6
    (C) 8
    (D) 9.5
    (E) 11

---

3. After an arrow is fired into the air, the arrow's height,
    $h(t)$, in feet over time, after t seconds, is modeled by the
    function $h(t) = -16t^2 + 160t + 4$. What statement best
    describes the meaning of $h(10.025) = 0$?

    (A) The arrow travels at 10.025 feet per second
    (B) The arrow gains 10.025 feet of height per second
    (C) The arrow reaches a maximum height of 10.025 feet
    (D) After 10.025 seconds, the arrow reaches its maximum
        height
    (E) After 10.025 seconds, the arrow falls to the ground

SSAT Functions

❑ On SSAT function problems, you will be asked to solve an equation using an unfamiliar symbol. The symbol represents the mathematical function to be carried out.

❑ Get comfortable with SSAT functions. The test writers have made up the symbols to confuse you. Don't panic when you encounter a weird symbol. Just plug in the numbers or variables you're given, and simplify the expression.

SSAT function questions will give you an equation that shows how the function works. Use this like a formula or a set of directions to follow for whatever values are put into the function.

> For all real numbers a and b, $a @ b = \dfrac{a+b}{ab}$. What does 5 @ 7 equal?
>
> In this question, $a = 5$, $b = 7$.
>
> Rewrite the expression, putting in a 5 for every a, and a 7 for every b:
>
> $5 @ 7 \Rightarrow \dfrac{5+7}{5 \times 7} \Rightarrow \dfrac{12}{35}$

TRY IT OUT

The following definition applies to questions 1-3.

For all real numbers A, B, and C, $\langle A, B, C \rangle = \dfrac{A+B}{C}$

The following definition applies to questions 4 and 5.

For all real numbers S, R, and T,

$$\triangle_{S}^{R\ T} = (S \times 3R) + (S \times 5T).$$

1. $\langle 2, 4, 1 \rangle =$

   (A) 4
   (B) 5
   (C) 6
   (D) 12
   (E) 16

2. What is the value of x, if $\langle x, 4, 10 \rangle = 1.4$?

   (A) 9
   (B) 10
   (C) 11
   (D) 12
   (E) 15

3. Which of the following must be true?

   I.   If $A = -B$, then $\langle A, B, C \rangle = 0$
   II. If $C = 0$, then $\langle A, B, C \rangle = 0$
   III. If $A = B = C$, then $\langle A, B, C \rangle = 2$

   (A) I only
   (B) II only
   (C) I and III only
   (D) II and III only
   (E) I, II, and III only

4. $\triangle_{0\ 1}^{2} =$

   (A) 0
   (B) 8
   (C) 10
   (D) 40
   (E) 450

5. If $\triangle_{n\ n}^{4} = 160$, what is the value of n?

   (A) 5
   (B) 10
   (C) 20
   (D) 40
   (E) None of the above.

PUT IT TOGETHER

1. If $[\![n]\!] = 2n^2 - 2$, then $[\![5]\!] =$

    (A) 18
    (B) 38
    (C) 48
    (D) 88
    (E) 98

Questions 2-3 are based on the following definition.

$$⇑x = x + 2 \text{ when } x \leq 4$$

$$⇑x = x - 3 \text{ when } x > 4$$

2. If $⇑3 = 5$ and $⇑⇑⇑3 = 2$, then $⇑⇑⇑⇑4 =$

    (A) 2
    (B) 3
    (C) 4
    (D) 5
    (E) 6

3. Which of the following is equal to 6?

    (A) $⇑⇑⇑1$
    (B) $⇑⇑⇑2$
    (C) $⇑⇑⇑3$
    (D) $⇑⇑⇑4$
    (E) $⇑⇑⇑5$

Questions 4-6 refer to the table in Figure 1.

For any two positive numbers x and y, $\langle x | y \rangle = \dfrac{x-2}{y-3}$

Example: $\langle 4 | 8 \rangle = \dfrac{4-2}{8-3} = \dfrac{2}{5}$

Figure 1

4. If $\langle m | n \rangle = 0$, what is the value of m?

    (A) 1
    (B) 2
    (C) 3
    (D) 4
    (E) 5

5. If $j = k$ and $\langle j | k \rangle = 2$, what is the value of k?

    (A) 7
    (B) 6
    (C) 5
    (D) 4
    (E) 3

6. For integers s and t, $\langle s | t \rangle$ can result in which of the following?

    I.   a positive integer
    II. a positive fraction
    III. a negative integer
    IV. a negative fraction
    V.   zero

    (A) I, II, and V only
    (B) I and III only
    (C) II and IV only
    (D) III, IV, and V only
    (E) I, II, III, IV, and V

Quadratic Equations

☐ **Factoring** – Factoring is expanding in reverse. Find common factors among the terms in an expression and rewrite using multiplication.

Factor:

$(x^2 + 3x + 2) = (x + 2)(x + 1)$

$(x^2 + 7x + 10) = $ _____

☐ **Factoring and Solving Quadratics** – Solve quadratic equations by following four simple steps:

1. Set the equation equal to zero.
2. Factor the equation.
3. Set each factor equal to zero.
4. Solve each of the resulting equations.

Solve for x: $x^2 + 8x = -7$

1. Set the equation equal to 0.

2. Factor the equation, looking for factors of 7 that have a sum of 8.

3. Set each expression equal to 0 and solve.

☐ Sometimes, you'll be able to use the common quadratics covered in the Algebraic Expressions module to simplify the factoring step.

$(a + b)^2 =$ $\qquad$ $(a + b)(a + b) = a^2 + ab + ba + b^2$ $\qquad$ $= a^2 + 2ab + b^2$

$(a - b)^2 =$ $\qquad$ $(a - b)(a - b) = a^2 - ab - ba + (-b)^2$ $\qquad$ $= a^2 - 2ab + b^2$

$(a + b)(a - b) =$ $\qquad$ $a^2 - ab + ba - b^2$ $\qquad$ $= a^2 - b^2$

Factor:

$x^2 - 16 = ($ _____ $)($ _____ $)$

TRY IT OUT

Factor:

1. $x^2 + 5x + 6$

2. $x^2 - 4x - 21$

3. $2x^2 + 5x + 2$

Solve for x:

4. $x^2 - 5x + 6$

5. $x^2 + x - 12$

6. $2x^2 + 6x + 4$

PUT IT TOGETHER

1. Which of the following is equivalent to $(2x + 9)(x - 4)$?

    (A) $2x^2 + x - 5$
    (B) $2x^2 + 5x - 5$
    (C) $2x^2 + x - 36$
    (D) $2x^2 + 5x - 36$
    (E) $2x^2 + 17x - 36$

---

2. What are the solutions to the equation $x^2 - 24 = -2x$?

    (A) -6 and -4
    (B) -6 and 4
    (C) -4 and 6
    (D) -3 and 8
    (E) -8 and 3

---

3. Which expression is equivalent to $2x^2 - 7x - 9$?

    (A) $(2x - 3)(x - 3)$
    (B) $(2x + 3)(x - 3)$
    (C) $(2x - 3)(x + 3)$
    (D) $(2x - 9)(x + 1)$
    (E) $(2x - 1)(x + 9)$

---

4. Which of the following is a solution to $3x^2 + 7x - 6 = 0$?

    (A) -2

    (B) $-\dfrac{2}{3}$

    (C) $\dfrac{2}{3}$

    (D) 2

    (E) 3

Checkpoint Review

1. Over the summer, Bobby watched 6 movies, and Henry watched *m* less than twice as many movies as Bobby did. In terms of *m*, how many movies did Henry watch?

    (A) $12 - 2m$
    (B) $12 - m$
    (C) $6 - 2m$
    (D) $m - 12$
    (E) $2m - 6$

2. Rebecca is *n* years old. John is twice as old as Rebecca was 3 years ago. How old is John in terms of *n*?

    (A) $2n - 6$
    (B) $2n - 3$
    (C) $n + 8$
    (D) $2n + 2$
    (E) $2n + 5$

3. The length, in words, of Stanley's essay is 147 less than three times the length of Colin's essay. Which of the following expressions best represents the length of Stanley's essay, in words, if Colin's essay is *x* words long?

    (A) $147 - (x + 3)$
    (B) $147 - 3x$
    (C) $147 + 3x$
    (D) $3x - 147$
    (E) $3x + 147$

4. If $f(x) = 2x^2 + 4$, then $f(2) + f(6) =$

    (A) 80
    (B) 88
    (C) 96
    (D) 160
    (E) 168

Checkpoint Review

5. If a piece of gum costs x cents, then how many pieces of gum can you buy with $3.00?

    (A) $3 - x$
    (B) $x - 3$
    (C) $3x$
    (D) $3 \div x$
    (E) $300 \div x$

    _____

6. What are the solutions to the equation $x^2 + 8x - 20 = 0$

    (A) $x = 5, 4$
    (B) $x = -5, 4$
    (C) $x = 5, -4$
    (D) $x = 10, -2$
    (E) $x = -10, 2$

    _____

7. Tara tosses a ball into the air. The ball's height, h, in feet over time, t, in seconds, can be modeled by the function $h = -2t^2 + 4t + 6$. After how many seconds does the ball fall to the ground?

    (A) 1
    (B) 2
    (C) 3
    (D) 4
    (E) 5

    _____

8. Which expression is equivalent to $(x^4 - 81)$?

    (A) $(x - 3)^4$
    (B) $(x^2 + 9)^2$
    (C) $(x^2 - 9)^2$
    (D) $(x - 3)^2(x + 3)^2$
    (E) $(x - 3)(x + 3)(x^2 + 9)$

Chapter Review

❑ Absolute Value

The absolute value of a number is the distance between the number and zero on the number line. Think of the absolute value of a number as the "positive value" of that number. To simplify an expression within an absolute value sign, simplify just as you would simplify an expression in parentheses. Then take the absolute value of the result.

❑ Scientific Notation

In "scientific notation," a number is written so that the largest digit is in the units place, and it is multiplied by a power of 10.

❑ Exponents

An exponent tells you how many times to multiply a number by itself. To multiply two numbers with the same base, add the exponents. To divide two numbers with the same base, subtract the exponents. To raise a power to a power, multiply the exponents.

❑ Roots

A square root (also known as a radical) is an exponent of 2 in reverse. A number's square root is the number which, when multiplied by itself, gives you the original number.

❑ Algebraic Expressions

Simplifying an algebraic expression is often the first step in solving an algebraic equation. To simplify an algebraic expression, combine similar terms. Use the distributive property to multiply a single term by an expression inside parentheses. When multiplying two binomials, each term must be multiplied by each term in the other binomial. Use the FOIL method: multiply the first terms, outside terms, inside terms, and last terms.

❑ Algebraic Equations

To solve an equation, get the variable by itself on one side of the equal sign. Keep the equation balanced. If you do something to one side, such as add a number or divide by a number, you must do the same to the other side. To solve an equation with a fraction, first get rid of the fraction by multiplying both sides of the equation by the denominator. To solve an equation with a radical sign, first get rid of the radical sign by isolating the radical on one side of the equation and then squaring both sides.

❑ Simultaneous Equations

Elimination Method – Add or subtract equations to cancel one of the variables and solve for the other. You may have to multiply an equation by some number to eliminate a variable before the equations are added or subtracted.

Substitution Method – Solve one equation for one of the variables, and then substitute that value for that variable in the other equation.

❑ Translating

Transforming words into mathematical equations is the first step in solving many SSAT problems. It is especially helpful in solving word problems. After reading the question, state in your own words what the problem is asking you to find. Break the problem into its parts and make certain you understand each of them. Translate the parts into "math language," and use the math equations you have set up to get the answer.

❑ Functions

A function is an "instruction" or "process" that for any value of x you put in will give you a single value of y (or $f(x)$) as a result. You can think of a function as a machine that takes inputs and converts them to outputs. You input a value for x, and the machine puts out a value for $f(x)$. To evaluate a function, $f(x)$, for a particular value of x, simply substitute that value everywhere you see an x.

❑ SSAT Functions

On SSAT function problems, you will be asked to solve an equation using an unfamiliar symbol. The symbol represents the mathematical function to be carried out.

❑ Quadratic Equations

Factoring is expanding in reverse. Find common factors among the terms in an expression and rewrite using multiplication. Solve quadratic equations by following four simple steps:

1. Set the equation equal to zero.
2. Factor the equation.
3. Set each factor equal to zero.
4. Solve each of the resulting equations.

Algebra Practice

Absolute Value

1. Which of the following is equivalent to $-2 \times |-3 - 4|$?

   (A) -14
   (B) -10
   (C) -2
   (D) 2
   (E) 14

---

2. Which of the following is equivalent to $|-2|^2 - |(-1)^3|$?

   (A) -5
   (B) -3
   (C) 3
   (D) 5
   (E) 7

Scientific Notation

3. Which of the following numbers is greatest in value?

   (A) $1,100,000 \times 10^{-2}$
   (B) $11,000,000 \times 10^{-4}$
   (C) 0.11×10^4
   (D) $110,000$
   (E) 0.0011×10^7

Exponents

4. 2.5^2 is closest to which of the following?

   (A) 8
   (B) 9
   (C) 10
   (D) 12
   (E) 15

---

5. What is the greatest common factor of $3y^{20}$ and $2x^2y^{12}$?

   (A) y^4
   (B) y^{12}
   (C) $2y^6$
   (D) $6y^4$
   (E) $6y^6$

Roots

6. What is the square root of 25?

    (A) 2.5
    (B) 4
    (C) 5
    (D) 50
    (E) 625

___

7. Which of the following does NOT equal 100?

    (A) 10^2
    (B) 10×10
    (C) 1×100
    (D) $1000 \div 10$
    (E) $\sqrt{1000}$

___

8. Which expression is equivalent to $\sqrt{75} + \sqrt{27}$?

    (A) $\sqrt{102}$
    (B) $34\sqrt{3}$
    (C) $15\sqrt{3}$
    (D) $8\sqrt{3}$
    (E) $2\sqrt{6}$

___

9. Which of the following is equivalent to $\sqrt{\dfrac{144x}{36}}$ when x equals 4?

    (A) 1
    (B) 2
    (C) 4
    (D) 8
    (E) 16

Algebraic Expressions

10. If x is a whole number, which of the following numbers can be written in the form $3x + 2$?

   (A) 54
   (B) 61
   (C) 72
   (D) 86
   (E) 93

11. Which of the following expressions is equivalent to $2x^2 - x - 3$?

   (A) $(2x - 3)(x + 1)$
   (B) $(2x + 3)(x + 1)$
   (C) $(2x - 3)(x - 1)$
   (D) $(2x - 1)(x + 3)$
   (E) $(2x + 3)(x + 3)$

12. Which of the following expressions is equivalent to $(2x + 1)(x^2 - 2x - 1)$?

   (A) $2x^3 - 3x^2 + 4x - 1$
   (B) $2x^3 - 3x^2 - 4x - 1$
   (C) $2x^3 - 5x^2 + 4x - 1$
   (D) $2x^3 - 5x^2 - 4x - 1$
   (E) $2x^3 - 5x^2 - 1$

13. Which of the following expressions is equivalent to $2x^2 - 5x - 1 + (x + 3)(x - 1)$?

   (A) $3x^2 - 3x + 2$
   (B) $3x^2 - 3x - 4$
   (C) $3x^2 - 3x + 3$
   (D) $3x^2 - 7x - 2$
   (E) $3x^2 - 7x + 2$

Algebraic Equations

14. If $2 \times (M + N) = 6$ and M is an integer, N could NOT be

    (A) -3
    (B) 0
    (C) 1
    (D) 1.5
    (E) 2

---

15. If $y = x + 1$, then which of the following is equal to $x - 3$?

    (A) $y + 4$
    (B) $y + 2$
    (C) $y - 2$
    (D) $y - 4$
    (E) It cannot be determined from the information given.

---

16. If $3 \times 8 \times y = 0$, then $y =$

    (A) -24
    (B) -11
    (C) 0
    (D) $\dfrac{1}{24}$
    (E) 1

---

17. If x and y are positive numbers and $\dfrac{(x - y)}{1} = 1$, which of

    the following must be true?

    (A) y is greater than x
    (B) $y = 1$
    (C) $x = y$
    (D) $y = x + 1$
    (E) $x = y + 1$

---

18. What is the value of x if $(7x + 4) - (3x - 1) = 61$?

    (A) 14
    (B) 14.5
    (C) 16
    (D) 16.5
    (E) 18

Inequalities

19. M is a whole number less than 11 and greater than 5.
    Which of the following CANNOT be M?

    (A) 10
    (B) 9
    (C) 8
    (D) 7.5
    (E) 6

20. If $x \leq 3$, then $x + 2$ must be less than or equal to

    (A) 1
    (B) 2
    (C) 3
    (D) 4
    (E) 5

21. If $x + 2$ is greater than 5, then $3x$ could be which of the
    following?

    (A) 1
    (B) 2
    (C) 6
    (D) 9
    (E) 15

Simultaneous Equations

22. If $4x + 3y = -1$ and $2x + y = -3$, what is the value of y?

    (A) –5
    (B) –4
    (C) –1
    (D) 4
    (E) 5

23. At a clothing store, 3 dresses and 2 pants cost $202, and 2
    dresses and 4 pants cost $212. What is the cost of 1 dress?

    (A) $28
    (B) $29
    (C) $48
    (D) $49
    (E) $64

Translating

24. When 12 is divided by a number, the result is 6. When the same number is increased by 10, the result is

    (A) 4
    (B) 8
    (C) 10
    (D) 12
    (E) 16

---

25. If 5 times N is 20, then 5 times $N + 1$ is

    (A) 15
    (B) 25
    (C) 30
    (D) 60
    (E) 105

---

26. It took Alice 45 minutes to complete her math homework. It took Diane t minutes to complete her science homework. What is the total amount of time that Alice and Diane spent on their homework?

    (A) 45 minutes
    (B) t minutes
    (C) $45 + t$ minutes
    (D) $45 \times t$ minutes
    (E) $45 - t$ minutes

---

27. For every hammer in a shop, there are between 6 and 8 screwdrivers. If there are y hammers in the shop, what is the largest number of hammers and screwdrivers that could be in the shop?

    (A) $8y + 8$
    (B) $y + 8$
    (C) $8y + 6$
    (D) $9y$
    (E) $14y$

Functions

28. For function $f(x) = -x^2 + 5x$, what is the value of $f(-4)$?

    (A) 36
    (B) 32
    (C) 4
    (D) –4
    (E) –36

29. If $f(x) = x + 9$ and $g(x) = x^3 - 19$, what is the value of

    $\dfrac{f(3)}{g(3)}$?

    (A) 0.75
    (B) 0.8
    (C) 1
    (D) 1.2
    (E) 1.5

30.
$$f(x) = 8x + 33$$

    For the function f defined above, $f(p) = 1$. What is the value of p?

    (A) 41
    (B) 3
    (C) –1
    (D) –4
    (E) –32

31. The distance, d, in meters, of a freight train from a train station over time, in t seconds, is modeled by the function $d(t) = -10t + 600$. What statement best describes the meaning of $d(60) = 0$?

    (A) After 1 minute, the train will reach the station.
    (B) The train has been traveling away from the station for 1 minute.
    (C) Over 1 minute, the train accelerates to 10 meters per second.
    (D) When the train stops, it will be 60 meters from the station.
    (E) When the train started moving, it was 60 meters from the station.

SSAT Functions

32. $R \rightarrow 1 = R$
        $R \rightarrow 2 = 2R + R$
        $R \rightarrow 3 = 3R + 2R + R$

Following the pattern above, $R \rightarrow 4 =$

(A) $5R$
(B) $6R$
(C) $7R$
(D) $9R$
(E) $10R$

33. Let a function be defined by $f(x \dagger y) = 2xy - y$. What is the value of $f(3 \dagger -8)$?

(A) −16
(B) −32
(C) −40
(D) −48
(E) −56

Questions 34 – 35 refer to the following definition.

For all real numbers r and s, $r \Diamond s = (r \times s) + (r - s)$

For example, $8 \Diamond 4 = (8 \times 4) + (8 - 4) = 32 + 4 = 36$

34. $5 \Diamond 2 =$

(A) 3
(B) 5
(C) 10
(D) 13
(E) 17

35. If $N \Diamond 3 = 29$, then $N =$

(A) 2
(B) 8
(C) 9
(D) 26
(E) 32

Quadratic Equations

36. Which expression is equivalent to $x^2 + x - 12$?

   (A) $(x + 12)(x - 1)$
   (B) $(x - 12)(x - 1)$
   (C) $(x + 4)(x - 3)$
   (D) $(x + 3)(x - 4)$
   (E) $(x + 2)(x - 6)$

37. What are the solutions to the equation $x^2 - x - 2 = 0$?

   (A) $-2, -1$
   (B) $-2, 0$
   (C) $-2, 1$
   (D) $2, -1$
   (E) $2, 1$

38. Which expression is equivalent to $2x^2 + 7x - 4$?

   (A) $(2x - 1)(x + 4)$
   (B) $(2x + 1)(x - 4)$
   (C) $(2x - 1)(x - 3)$
   (D) $(2x - 2)(x + 2)$
   (E) $(2x + 2)(x - 2)$

39. Which expression is equivalent to the expression
    $(5x^2 + x - 11) - (4x^2 - 3x - 14)$?

   (A) $(x + 1)(x + 3)$
   (B) $(x + 1)(x - 3)$
   (C) $(x - 1)(x + 3)$
   (D) $(x - 2)(x - 2)$
   (E) $(x + 2)(x + 2)$

40. If $x^2 + x + 2 = (x + 2)(x - 1) + n$, then $n =$

   (A) 0
   (B) 1
   (C) 2
   (D) 3
   (E) 4

Algebra Practice – Middle Level

1. If $63,072 = 20,000 + 43,010 + N$, then $N =$

   (A) 9
   (B) 59
   (C) 62
   (D) 69
   (E) 72

2. If $3N = 24$, then $9N =$

   (A) 24
   (B) 27
   (C) 32
   (D) 48
   (E) 72

3. If $\dfrac{5}{6} = \dfrac{x}{24}$, then $x =$

   (A) 10
   (B) 15
   (C) 20
   (D) 24
   (E) 27

4. $7(1 + 10 + 100) = 420 + 57 + \Phi$. What does Φ equal?

   (A) –6
   (B) 6
   (C) 300
   (D) 366
   (E) 400

5. If $40x = 800,000$, what is $x?$

   (A) 2
   (B) 200
   (C) 2,000
   (D) 20,000
   (E) 200,000

6. If $\dfrac{100}{25} + \dfrac{70}{25} + \dfrac{A}{25} = 7$, what is A?

    (A) 0
    (B) 2
    (C) 5
    (D) 15
    (E) 25

7. When $x - 6 = 0$, what is the value of x?

    (A) –6
    (B) 6
    (C) x
    (D) 0
    (E) It cannot be determined from the information given.

8. If $100 + N = 110$, then $101 \times N =$

    (A) 10
    (B) 101
    (C) 202
    (D) 1,010
    (E) 4,001

9. If $200 \div q = 10$, what is q?

    (A) 2
    (B) 10
    (C) 20
    (D) 100
    (E) 200

10. How many months are there in M years?

    (A) M
    (B) $M \times 12$
    (C) $M \times 100$
    (D) $100 \div M$
    (E) 100

11. N is a whole number. If $3N + 8 < 40$, what is the greatest possible value of N?

(A) 9
(B) 10
(C) 11
(D) 12
(E) 13

12. The sum of 3 consecutive integers is 4 times the smallest number. What is the largest number?

(A) 3
(B) 4
(C) 5
(D) 6
(E) 7

13. Let $\therefore N$ be defined as followed for all integers N:

$\therefore N = 2N$ if N is even.

$\therefore N = 3N$ if N is odd.

What is the value of $(\therefore 50) + (\therefore 1)$?

(A) 51
(B) 102
(C) 103
(D) 152
(E) 153

14. If $2N + 5 = N + 30$, then $N =$

(A) 10
(B) 15
(C) 20
(D) 25
(E) 30

15. If $y = 8$, then $(y - 1)^2 =$

(A) 81
(B) 64
(C) 49
(D) 36
(E) 25

16. *A* is less than 1, but greater than 0. Which of the following must be true?

(A) $3A < 1$

(B) $\dfrac{1}{A} < 1$

(C) $A > \dfrac{1}{A}$

(D) $A > A^2$

(E) $A + 1 < 1$

17. If $151 - A = 150$, then $150 \times A =$

(A) 0

(B) $\dfrac{1}{151}$

(C) 1

(D) 150

(E) 151

18. What is $2N$ if $\dfrac{1}{2}N = 15$?

(A) 5

(B) 15

(C) 30

(D) 45

(E) 60

19. $12\square + 210 = \square\square\square$, where $\square$ is a digit. What digit does $\square$ represent?

(A) 0

(B) 1

(C) 2

(D) 3

(E) 12

20. If $15 \times 13 = (100 \times 1) + (10 \times 9)\,(1 \times \Omega)$, what is the value of Ω?

(A) 1

(B) 3

(C) 4

(D) 5

(E) 6

21. If $|2x - 7| = 5$, what are all of the solutions for x?

    (A) $-1, -6$
    (B) $1, 6, -6$
    (C) $1, -6$
    (D) $1, 6$
    (E) 1

22. Write 0.000000106 in scientific notation:

    (A) $.106 \times 10^{-7}$
    (B) $.106 \times 10^{-8}$
    (C) 1.06×10^{-7}
    (D) 1.06×10^{-8}
    (E) 10.6×10^{-6}

23. What is the greatest integer less than $\sqrt{80}$?

    (A) 7
    (B) 8
    (C) 9
    (D) 10
    (E) 11

24. Which of the following gives the best approximation for the number of days in w weeks, m months, and y years?

    (A) $\dfrac{w}{7} + \dfrac{m}{30} + \dfrac{y}{365}$

    (B) $\dfrac{7}{w} + \dfrac{30}{m} + \dfrac{365}{y}$

    (C) $365y + 30m + 7w$
    (D) $y + 12m + 52w$
    (E) $y + m + w$

25. If $f(x) = 6x - 10$, then $f(3) - f(2) =$

    (A) 1
    (B) 4
    (C) 6
    (D) 10
    (E) 16

Algebra Practice – Upper Level

1. 3 less than 4 times a number is 17. What is the number?

   (A) 2
   (B) 5
   (C) 12
   (D) 20
   (E) 51

2. Which value of N does NOT satisfy $\dfrac{N}{4}+\dfrac{2}{3}>\dfrac{1}{6}$?

   (A) 2
   (B) 1
   (C) 0
   (D) –1
   (E) –2

3. If $M > 2$, then $2M + 2$ CANNOT be

   (A) 14
   (B) 12
   (C) 10
   (D) 8
   (E) 6

4. If $\dfrac{37}{A}=A\times 37$, what is the value of $A \times A$?

   (A) $\dfrac{1}{1,369}$
   (B) 1
   (C) 1,369
   (D) $\dfrac{1}{37}$
   (E) 37

5. If $m + 5 = 10$ and $n - 6 = 3$, then $m \times n =$

   (A) 54
   (B) 45
   (C) 35
   (D) 14
   (E) 11

6. Juan scored $N - 5$ points in the basketball game. Seth scored 2 more points than Juan. How many points did Seth score?

   (A) $N - 7$
   (B) $N - 5$
   (C) $N - 3$
   (D) N
   (E) $N + 7$

7. If $(A + B) \div 6 > 2$, and A is equal to 7, B could be which of the following?

   (A) -3
   (B) 0
   (C) 4
   (D) $4\frac{1}{2}$
   (E) 6

8. If $6y = 2x + 6$, then which of the following equals $3y$?

   (A) x
   (B) $6 - x$
   (C) $x + 3$
   (D) $x + 6$
   (E) $2x + 3$

9. If P is an integer, $4P - 1$ could be which of the following?

   (A) 10
   (B) 11
   (C) 12
   (D) 13
   (E) 14

10. If $245 = (2 \times A) + (4 \times B) + (5 \times C)$, which of the following could be true?

    (A) $A = 10, B = 1, C = 0$
    (B) $A = 10, B = 10, C = 10$
    (C) $A = 1, B = 1, C = 1$
    (D) $A = 100, B = 10, C = 1$
    (E) $A = 1, B = 10, C = 100$

11. If $3x < 9$, which of the following is a possible value of x?

   (A) 27
   (B) 9
   (C) 4.5
   (D) 3
   (E) 2

12. 500 books make up a collection. 125 books make up a bookshelf. 34 books make up a hobby. How many books are represented by c collections, b bookshelves, and 2 hobbies?

   (A) $\dfrac{c+b+2h}{500+125+34}$

   (B) $500c + 125b + 17h$

   (C) $\dfrac{a}{500} + \dfrac{b}{125} + \dfrac{2h}{34}$

   (D) $500c + 125b + 34h$

   (E) $500c + 125b + 68$

13. In one year, Bill will be three times as old as Monica. If Monica is M years old now, how old is Bill now?

   (A) $3M + 2$
   (B) $3M - 3$
   (C) $3M - 1$
   (D) $3M + 3$
   (E) $\dfrac{M+1}{3}$

14. The product of 1 less than r and 3 more than r equals 12. Which of the following could be a value for r?

   (A) 1
   (B) 2
   (C) 3
   (D) 4
   (E) 5

15. A laborer earns a salary of x dollars. A supervisor earns $10,000 more than a laborer. A manager earns $2,000 less than five times what a supervisor earns. Which expression represents a manager's salary in dollars?

    (A) $x + 52,000$
    (B) $5x + 48,000$
    (C) $5x + 52,000$
    (D) $10x + 48,000$
    (E) $10x + 52,000$

16. Which represents the solution of $9 - 2y < 17 - 2x$ in terms of y?

    (A) $y > x + 7$
    (B) $y < x + 4$
    (C) $y > x + 4$
    (D) $y < x - 4$
    (E) $y > x - 4$

17. If $f(x) = 4x - 9$ and $f(m) = 9$, what is the value of m?

    (A) 0
    (B) $\dfrac{1}{4}$
    (C) $\dfrac{1}{2}$
    (D) 4
    (E) $4\dfrac{1}{2}$

18. $3x + 2y = 5$

                        $5x + 3y = 6$

    For the system of equations above, what is the value of x?

    (A) -7
    (B) -3
    (C) 3
    (D) 6
    (E) 7

19. What are the solutions to the equation $x^2 + 2x - 24 = 0$?

    (A) $-1, 24$
    (B) $-3, 8$
    (C) $-6, 4$
    (D) $-8, 3$
    (E) $-12, 2$

20. If $(x^3)(x^{y+1}) = x^{12}$, what is the value of y?

    (A) $2\frac{2}{3}$

    (B) 3

    (C) $3\frac{2}{3}$

    (D) 4
    (E) 8

21. If $x < -5$, then $|x + 5|$ is equal to which of the following?

    (A) 0
    (B) $x + 5$
    (C) $x - 5$
    (D) $-x - 5$
    (E) $-x + 5$

22. A whole number is represented by the variable n. What is the least possible value of n if $7n > 400$?

    (A) 57
    (B) 58
    (C) 67
    (D) 77
    (E) 78

23. What is the product of the cube root of -8 and the square root of 121?

    (A) 22
    (B) 13
    (C) 9
    (D) -9
    (E) -22

24. Which expression is equivalent to $2x^2 + 7x - 15$?

    (A) $(2x + 5)(x - 3)$
    (B) $(2x - 5)(x - 3)$
    (C) $(2x - 5)(x + 3)$
    (D) $(2x - 3)(x - 5)$
    (E) $(2x - 3)(x + 5)$

25. If $f(x) = 3x - 2$, then $f(x + 1) =$

    (A) $3x + 1$
    (B) $3x^2 - 2x - 2$
    (C) $3x^2 + x - 2$
    (D) $3x - 1$
    (E) $3x^2 - 2x - 1$

SUMMIT
EDUCATIONAL
GROUP

Geometry

❏ Angles   216

❏ Parallel Lines   220

❏ Triangles   222

❏ Area and Perimeter   228

❏ Circles   236

❏ Volume   240

❏ Spatial Reasoning   242

❏ Coordinate Plane   246

❏ Midpoint & Distance   248

❏ Transformations   250

❏ Slope   252

❏ Graphing Lines   254

Geometry

❑ About one-fifth of SSAT math is geometry. In general, the geometric concepts you need to know deal with angle measurement, perimeter, and area.

❑ In this chapter, you will:

- study the basic geometric concepts of angles, perimeter, area, volume, and parallel lines.
- learn different strategies for attacking SSAT geometry problems.

Vocabulary

❑ To **bisect** means to divide into two equal parts.

❑ A **vertex** is a corner or a point where lines meet.

❑ **Perimeter** is the distance around the edge of a two-dimensional figure.

❑ **Area** is the measurement of the space inside a two-dimensional figure. Area is measured in square units.

❑ **Volume** is the amount of space occupied by a three-dimensional figure.

❑ **Coordinates** are the pairs of numbers which specify the position of points in a two-dimensional coordinate plane.

❑ It is important to understand common geometric symbols and notations.

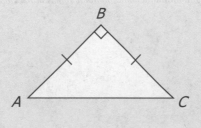

Triangles are denoted by the letter at their corners, or "vertices."

The triangle above is $\triangle ABC$.

Line segments are denoted by their endpoints.

The figure above contains line segments $\overline{AB}$, $\overline{BC}$, and $\overline{AC}$.

Tick marks are used to indicate line segments of equal length.

In the figure above, $AB = BC$.

90° angles are indicated by a small square at the vertex.

Angles are denoted by the vertex, or by three points with the vertex in the middle.

In the figure above, $\angle B = 90°$, or $\angle ABC = 90°$.

Angles

❏ A **right angle** has a measure of 90°. This is indicated by a square drawn at the vertex. The lines that form the right angle are **perpendicular**. The symbol for perpendicular is ⊥.

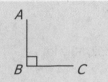

$\angle ABC = 90°$

$AB \perp BC$

❏ A **straight line** is a 180° angle.

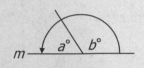

Line m has a measure of 180°.

Notice that $a + b = 180°$.

❏ **Circle**:

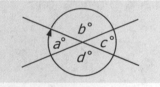

$a + b + c + d =$ _____

❏ **Vertical Angles**:

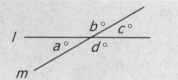

$a =$ ____ ; $b =$ ____

❏ **Triangle**:

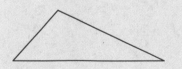

$x + y + z =$ _____

❏ **Quadrilateral**:

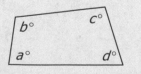

$a + b + c + d =$ _____

SUMMIT
EDUCATIONAL
GROUP

❑ The sum of the interior angles of any polygon = $(n - 2) \times 180°$, where n is the number of sides.

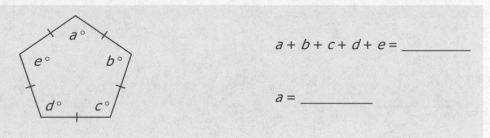

$a + b + c + d + e =$ _____

$a =$ _____

❑ Label all angles in figures as described in the questions. Calculate and label other angles as well. If the figure is not provided, draw one and label it!

❑ Unless a problem says differently, all figures are drawn to scale. On figures that are drawn to scale, you can sometimes narrow down your answer choices by estimating angles.

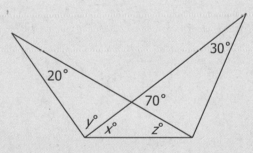

In the figure above, if $y = 2x$, $z =$

(A) 25
(B) 45
(C) 55
(D) 65
(E) 70

This problem is difficult, but estimation is a helpful strategy.
Angle z looks like it is less than half of a right angle, so it is likely less than 45°.
(A) is the only answer choice less than 45, and it is the correct answer.

TRY IT OUT

Guess the measures of each of these four angles:

1.

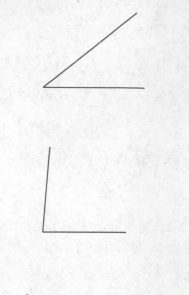

2.

3.

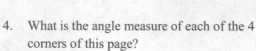

4. What is the angle measure of each of the 4 corners of this page?

5. How many degrees are in a third of a circle?

6. If the hands of a watch read 5:00, what is the measure of the angle formed by the hands?

7. Draw a line from the upper right corner of this page down to the lower left corner. Estimate the measures of the angles formed by this line and the edges of the page.

8. In the figure below, $x =$

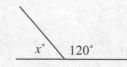

9. In the figure below, if $x = 35°$, what does y equal?

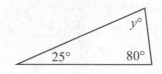

10. In the figure below, $y =$

11. In the figure below, $y =$

12. In the figure below, $y =$

PUT IT TOGETHER

1. If two of the angles of a triangle are 56° and 42°, then the third angle is

    (A) 82°
    (B) 89°
    (C) 98°
    (D) 102°
    (E) 149°

2.

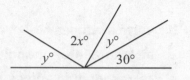

    If four lines meet as shown in the figure, what is the value of $x + y$?

    (A) 50
    (B) 60
    (C) 75
    (D) 150
    (E) It cannot be determined from the information given.

---

3. What is the measure of each angle in a regular octagon?

    (A) 45
    (B) 75
    (C) 105
    (D) 135
    (E) 150

4.

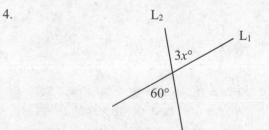

    In the figure shown above, $x =$

    (A) 20
    (B) 40
    (C) 60
    (D) 180
    (E) 36

Parallel Lines

Parallel line questions typically present a diagram – parallelograms, trapezoids, and a variety of parallel lines cut by a transversal – and require a solid understanding of which angles are equal and which are supplementary.

❏ When a line crosses through parallel lines, it creates several sets of equal angles and supplementary angles. The "big" angles are equal and the "small" angles are equal. The sum of a "big" angle and a "small" angle is 180°.

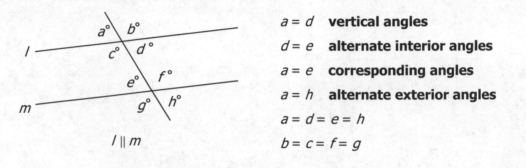

$a = d$ **vertical angles**

$d = e$ **alternate interior angles**

$a = e$ **corresponding angles**

$a = h$ **alternate exterior angles**

$a = d = e = h$

$b = c = f = g$

❏ When a problem contains parallel lines, identify and label all equal angles. Calculate any remaining angles where possible. If a figure is not drawn, draw one!

If $l \parallel m$, and one angle is given as shown, label the unmarked angles in the figure below.

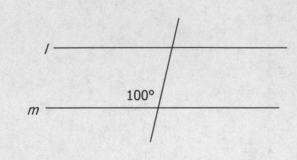

❏ A **parallelogram** is a quadrilateral in which opposite sides are parallel and opposite sides and angles are equal. A **trapezoid** is a quadrilateral in which one pair of opposite sides is parallel. If the non-parallel sides of a trapezoid are equal in length, then the figure is called an **isosceles trapezoid**.

Questions with parallelograms and trapezoids are often parallel line questions. Use your parallel line and angle rules to calculate all the angles.

TRY IT OUT

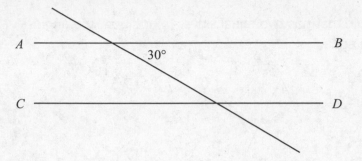

In the figure above, $AB \parallel CD$. Fill in the missing angles in the figure above.

PUT IT TOGETHER

1.

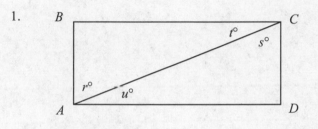

In the figure above, if $ABCD$ is a rectangle, which of the following must be true?

(A) $r = t$
(B) $r = u$
(C) $r = 45°$
(D) $t = u$
(E) $u = s$

2.

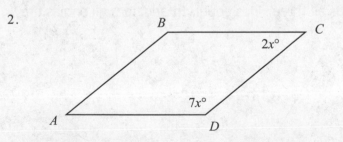

In the figure above, if $ABCD$ is a parallelogram, what is the value of x?

(A) 180
(B) 140
(C) 40
(D) 20
(E) 10

Isosceles & Equilateral Triangles

❑ An isosceles triangle is any triangle that has two equal sides. In addition, the angles opposite the congruent sides are equal.

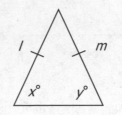

$l = m$ and $x = y$

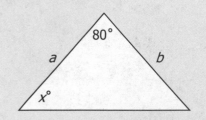

If $a = b$, what is the value of x?

> Since sides a and b are equal, the triangle must be isosceles. Therefore, the angles opposite a and b must be equal. The angles of the triangle must be 80°, $x°$, and $x°$. Since the sum of the angles of a triangle is always 180°, we know that $80 + x + x = 180$.
>
> $80 + 2x = 180$ ⟹ $2x = 100$ ⟹ $x = 50$

❑ An equilateral triangle is a triangle that has all three sides equal. In addition, all angles are 60°.

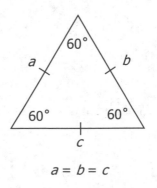

$a = b = c$

TRY IT OUT

Fill in the missing angles of the two triangles below:

1.

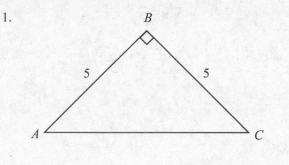

2.

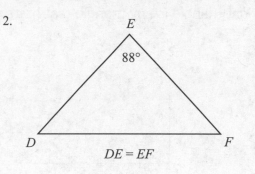

$DE = EF$

PUT IT TOGETHER

1.

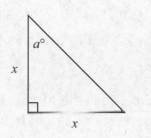

In the figure shown above, what is the value of a?

(A) 30
(B) 45
(C) 60
(D) 90
(E) It cannot be determined from the information given.

2.

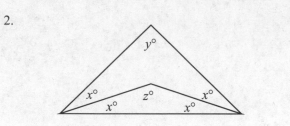

Note: Figure not drawn to scale.

In the figure shown above, if $z = 4x$, what is the value of y?

(A) 30
(B) 45
(C) 60
(D) 72
(E) 90

Right Triangles

❑ A right triangle is any triangle that has a 90° angle as one of its angles.

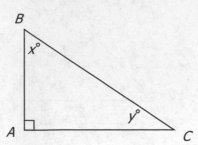

△*ABC* is a right triangle because ∠*BAC* is a right angle.

Note: The sum of the two non-right angles in a right triangle is 90°. In the triangle above, $x + y = 90°$.

❑ The two sides that form the right angle are the **legs**. The third side is the **hypotenuse**. The hypotenuse is opposite the right angle, and it is the longest side of a right triangle.

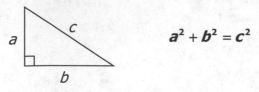

❑ The **Pythagorean Theorem** states that in any right triangle the square of the hypotenuse is equal to the sum of the squares of the other two sides.

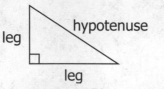

$$a^2 + b^2 = c^2$$

Find the value of *x*:

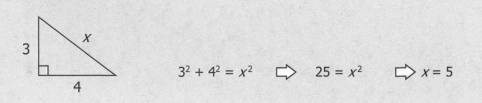

$3^2 + 4^2 = x^2$ ⇨ $25 = x^2$ ⇨ $x = 5$

TRY IT OUT

Try the following:

1. How do you know that the sum of the two non-right angles of a right triangle is 90°?

2.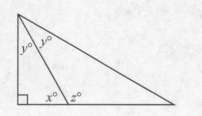

    In the figure above, what is the value of x?

PUT IT TOGETHER

1. In a right isosceles triangle the three angles are

    (A) 45°, 45°, 90°
    (B) 30°, 60°, 90°
    (C) 40°, 40°, 100°
    (D) 60°, 60°, 60°
    (E) 50°, 50°, 100°

2.

    In the figure shown above, if $z = 2x$, which of the following gives the value of y in terms of z?

    (A) $\dfrac{z}{2}$

    (B) $\dfrac{z}{3}$

    (C) $90 - \dfrac{z}{2}$

    (D) $180 - \dfrac{z}{2}$

    (E) $180 - z$

Checkpoint Review

1.

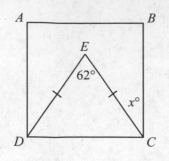

The figure above shows square *ABCD* and isosceles triangle *CDE*. What is the value of *x*?

(A) 21
(B) 29
(C) 31
(D) 39
(E) 41

2. Two of the angles of a parallelogram measure $8x°$ and $7x°$. What is the value of *x*?

(A) 12
(B) 16
(C) 18
(D) 24
(E) 32

3. In the figure shown below, line *l* is parallel to line *m*. What is the value of *x*?

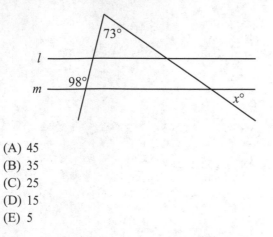

(A) 45
(B) 35
(C) 25
(D) 15
(E) 5

Checkpoint Review

4. One angle of an isosceles triangle measures 44°. Which of the following could be the measure of another angle in the triangle?

    (A) 136°
    (B) 92°
    (C) 79°
    (D) 78°
    (E) 46°

5.

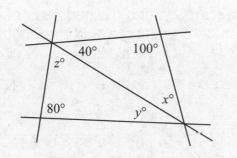

In the figure above, the measures of three angles are shown. What is the value of $x + y + z$?

    (A) 180
    (B) 140
    (C) 120
    (D) 100
    (E) 60

6.

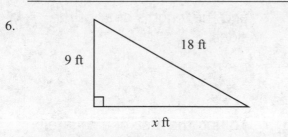

In the figure above, what is the value of x?

    (A) $\sqrt{324 + 81}$
    (B) $\sqrt{324 - 81}$
    (C) $\sqrt{324} - \sqrt{81}$
    (D) $\sqrt{18 - 9}$
    (E) $\sqrt{18} - \sqrt{9}$

Area & Perimeter – Rectangle & Square

❑ **Perimeter** is the distance around the edge of a two-dimensional figure.

❑ **Area** is the measurement of the space inside a two-dimensional figure. Area is measured in square units.

❑ A **rectangle** is a 4-sided figure with 4 right angles. In a rectangle, opposite sides are equal.

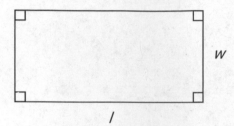

Perimeter To find the perimeter of a rectangle, add the lengths of all of the sides.

$$\text{Perimeter} = l + l + w + w = (2 \times l) + (2 \times w)$$

Area To find the area of a rectangle, multiply the length by the width.

$$\text{Area} = l \times w$$

❑ A **square** is a rectangle that has 4 equal sides.

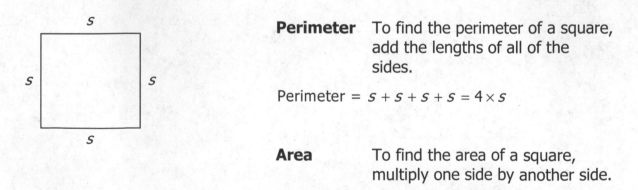

Perimeter To find the perimeter of a square, add the lengths of all of the sides.

$$\text{Perimeter} = s + s + s + s = 4 \times s$$

Area To find the area of a square, multiply one side by another side.

$$\text{Area} = s \times s$$

The rectangle above is divided into squares each 1 inch by 1 inch.

What is the perimeter of the rectangle? What is the area?

To find the perimeter, we need the length and width. If we placed a ruler along the top edge of the rectangle and measured, we'd get 6 inches. (There are 6 squares along the top edge and each square has a length of 1 inch.) Similarly, for the width, we'd get 4 inches. Therefore, the perimeter of the rectangle is 6 + 6 + 4 + 4 = 20 inches.

The area is the space inside the rectangle measured in square units. One way to calculate the area is to count the squares. Each square is a square unit. Specifically, each square is one square inch. There are 24 squares (or square inches), so the area of the rectangle is 24 square inches.

A quicker way to calculate the area is to use the formula for area of a rectangle and multiply the length times the width. The length is 6 and the width is 4 so we get $6 \times 4 = 24$ square inches.

TRY IT OUT

Find the area and perimeter of the square and rectangle below:

1.

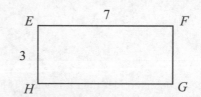

ABCD is a square.

AB = 2

Perimeter of *ABCD* =

Area of *ABCD* =

2.

Area of *EFGH* =

Perimeter of *EFGH* =

PUT IT TOGETHER

1.

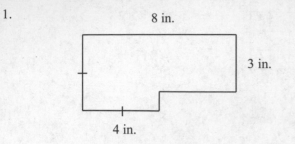

Find the perimeter of the irregular shape in the figure above.

(A) 15 in.
(B) 19 in.
(C) 23 in.
(D) 24 in.
(E) 26 in.

2.

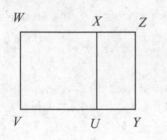

In the figure shown, if *UVWX* is a square, the length of *VY* is 9, and the length of *VW* is 6, what is the area of rectangular region *YUXZ*?

(A) 15
(B) 18
(C) 27
(D) 36
(E) 54

3. A rectangle is 2 centimeters longer than it is wide. If the perimeter is 28 centimeters, what is the area of the rectangle, in square centimeters?

(A) 196
(B) 192
(C) 162
(D) 56
(E) 48

4. In the figure below, *X* is a rectangular sheet of paper with a perimeter of 39 inches. *Y* shows the same sheet of paper after four squares, each with an area of 1 square inch, have been cut from the corners. What is the perimeter of the sheet of paper after it is cut?

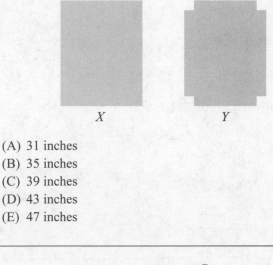

    X   Y

    (A) 31 inches
    (B) 35 inches
    (C) 39 inches
    (D) 43 inches
    (E) 47 inches

5.

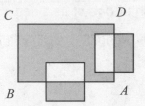

    In the figure above, rectangle *ABCD* has width 3 and length 5, and *AB* and *AD* bisect two squares, both with sides of length 2. What is the total area of the shaded regions?

    (A) 15
    (B) 16
    (C) 17
    (D) 18
    (E) 19

---

6. What is the greatest number of square blocks, 2 inches on each side, that can be placed into a storage box 13 inches long and 5 inches wide if no blocks can be stacked on top of each other?

    (A) 65
    (B) 48
    (C) 32
    (D) 16
    (E) 12

Area & Perimeter – Triangle

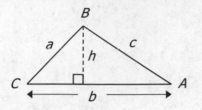

❑ To find the perimeter of a triangle, add the lengths of all of the sides.

Perimeter of $\triangle ABC = a + b + c$

❑ To find the area of a triangle, use the following formula:

$A = \dfrac{1}{2}bh$, where A = area, b = base, and h = height.

Note: The height of a triangle is not always the length of one of its sides.

The height must be perpendicular from the base of the triangle.

TRY IT OUT

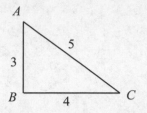

1.   What is the perimeter of △*ABC* above?

2.   What is the perimeter of an equilateral triangle that has one side of length 2?

3.   The perimeter of an equilateral triangle is 18. What are the lengths of the sides of the triangle?

Find the area of each triangle below.

4.

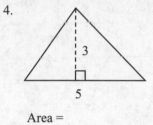

Area =

5.

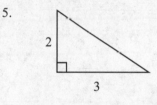

Area =

PUT IT TOGETHER

1.

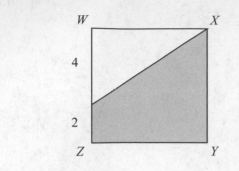

In the figure shown, if *WXYZ* is a square, what is the area of the shaded region?

(A) 30
(B) 24
(C) 18
(D) 16
(E) 12

2.

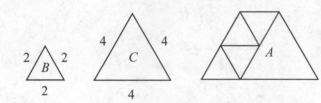

In the figure shown, shape *A* was made from shapes *B* and *C*. What is the perimeter of shape *A*?

(A) 36
(B) 32
(C) 28
(D) 16
(E) 14

3. What is the area, in square feet, of a right triangle which has a perimeter of 24 feet, hypotenuse with length 10 feet, and a leg with length 8 feet?

(A) 6
(B) 12
(C) 24
(D) 36
(E) 48

4.

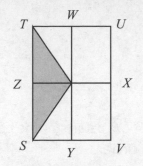

In the figure shown, W, X, Y, and Z are the midpoints of the line segments on which they lie. If A is the area of rectangular region $STUV$, what is the area of the shaded region, in terms of A?

(A) $\dfrac{A}{2}$

(B) $\dfrac{A}{4}$

(C) $\dfrac{A}{6}$

(D) $\dfrac{A}{8}$

(E) $\dfrac{3}{4}A$

5. The triangle shown has a perimeter of 18 inches. What is the area of the triangle?

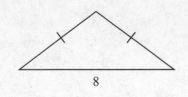

(A) 12
(B) 24
(C) $4\sqrt{39}$
(D) $4\sqrt{41}$
(E) 36

Circles

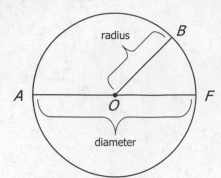

The **center** of the circle is located at *O*.

The **radius** of the circle ($\overline{OB}$) starts at the center and ends on the edge of the circle.

The **diameter** of the circle ($\overline{AF}$) cuts directly through the center of the circle and is twice the radius. All diameters have the same length.

❑ **Circumference** is the distance around the edge of the circle.

Circumference = $2 \times \pi \times r = \pi \times d$

❑ The **area** of a circle is found using the formula:

Area = $\pi \times r^2$

❑ Pi (π), is the ratio of a circle's diameter to its circumference.

The value of π is approximately 3.1416.

TRY IT OUT

Find the circumference of the circles below. Leave in terms of π.

1.

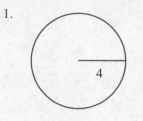

Radius = 4

Circumference =

2.

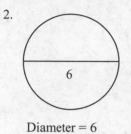

Diameter = 6

Circumference =

Find the area of each of the circles below:

3.

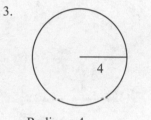

Radius = 4

Area =

4.

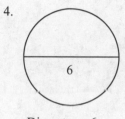

Diameter = 6

Area =

PUT IT TOGETHER

1.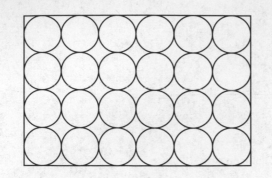

    24 coins are placed on the base of a rectangular display
    case as illustrated in the figure shown above. The radius
    of each coin is half an inch. Which of the following is the
    area, in square inches, of the base of the display case?

    (A) 6
    (B) 12
    (C) 24
    (D) 36
    (E) 48

2. What is the circumference, in terms of π yards, of a circle
    with an area of 24π square yards?

    (A) $2\pi\sqrt{6}$
    (B) $4\pi\sqrt{3}$
    (C) $4\pi\sqrt{6}$
    (D) $\sqrt{24\pi}$
    (E) $\sqrt{12\pi}$

3. Circle A has a radius of 6. If Circle B has a radius half the
    length of the radius of Circle A, then the circumference of
    Circle B is

    (A) π
    (B) 3π
    (C) 6π
    (D) 9π
    (E) 12π

4.

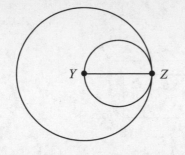

In the figure shown above, segment $\overline{YZ}$ is the diameter of the smaller circle and the radius of the larger circle. If the circumference of the smaller circle is 8π, what is the area of the larger circle?

(A) 8π
(B) 16π
(C) 32π
(D) 64π
(E) 256π

Volume

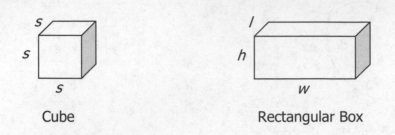

Cube　　　　　　　　　　Rectangular Box

❑ **Volume** is the amount of space occupied by a three-dimensional figure.

❑ Volume of a cube: $V = s^3$

❑ Volume of a rectangular box: $V = l \times w \times h$

❑ To calculate the **weight** of a figure, you must first know the weight of a cubic unit. Multiply that weight by the figure's volume of cubic units.

❑ **Capacity** is the amount that something can hold. Calculating the capacity of a figure is usually the same as calculating volume. Solid figures are typically used for volume questions, whereas capacity questions typically involve hollow figures that are being filled with something.

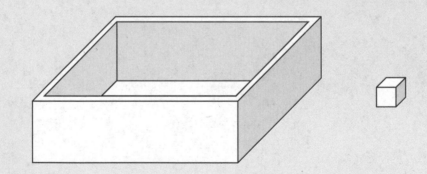

The inner dimensions of a box are 6 cm × 14 cm × 20 cm. How many cubes with a volume of 8 cm³ can fit inside this box?

What is the total volume of the inside of the box? _____

Divide this volume by the volume of a single cube: _____

TRY IT OUT

Find the volume of the cube and rectangular box below:

1.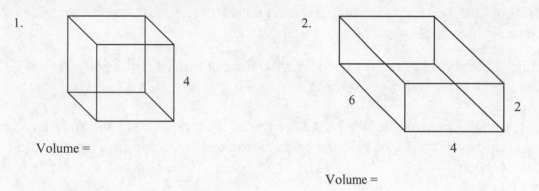

Volume =

2.

Volume =

PUT IT TOGETHER

1. The figure below shows a rectangular metal block. If the metal block were cut into two rectangular blocks of equal dimensions, which of the following could be the dimensions, in inches, of each of the smaller blocks?

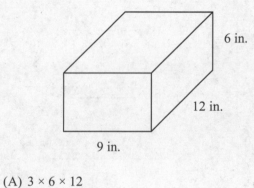

6 in.

12 in.

9 in.

(A) $3 \times 6 \times 12$
(B) $3 \times 6 \times 9$
(C) $3 \times 12 \times 9$
(D) $6 \times 3 \times 6$
(E) $6 \times 6 \times 6$

---

2. A cylinder has a diameter half its height and a volume of 108π in^3. What is the length, in inches, of the cylinder's radius? (volume of a cylinder $= \pi r^2 h$)

(A) 3
(B) 6
(C) 9
(D) 12
(E) 18

Spatial Reasoning

❑ Spatial reasoning questions test your problem-solving skills and your ability to visualize 2-dimensional and 3-dimensional situations.

   These questions do not typically require strong math skills, but instead require strong reasoning, thoroughness, and some cleverness.

❑ During the test, use anything available to help solve spatial reasoning questions. You may be able to use your pencil, hands, or even the pages of the test booklet to help imagine the situation in the question.

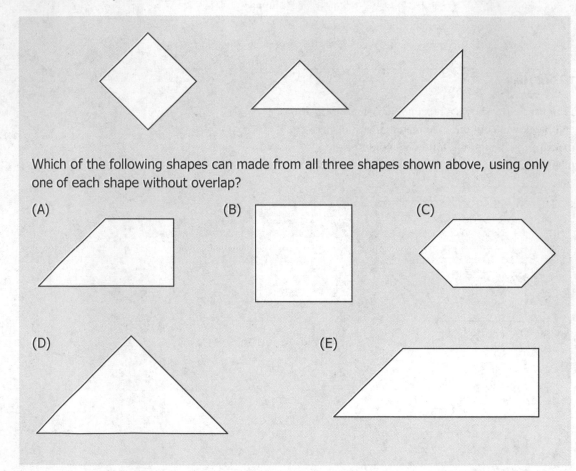

Which of the following shapes can made from all three shapes shown above, using only one of each shape without overlap?

(A)　　　　　　　　　　(B)　　　　　　　　　　(C)

(D)　　　　　　　　　　(E)

PUT IT TOGETHER

1.

The figure above shows 9 stacks of blocks. If the blocks are all the same size and shape and they are stacked on a level base, what is the total number of blocks in the 9 stacks?

(A) 48
(B) 46
(C) 38
(D) 35
(E) 23

2. How many quadrilaterals are there in the figure shown?

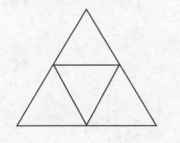

(A) 0
(B) 3
(C) 5
(D) 6
(E) 10

Checkpoint Review

1.

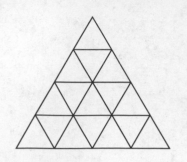

How many triangles are there in the figure shown above?

(A) 16
(B) 22
(C) 24
(D) 25
(E) 27

2.

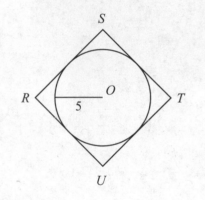

In the figure shown above, O is the center of the circle that has a radius of 5 meters. What is the area, in square meters, of square $RSTU$?

(A) 40
(B) 80
(C) 100
(D) 160
(E) 400

Checkpoint Review

3. Circle *X* has a radius of 6 inches and Circle *Y* has a diameter of 6 inches. What is the difference in the area, in square inches, of these two circles?

    (A) 0
    (B) 27π
    (C) 36π
    (D) 45π
    (E) 72π

4.

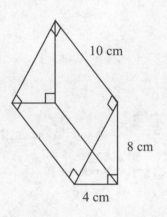

10 cm

8 cm

4 cm

What is the volume, in cubic centimeters, of the right triangular prism shown?

    (A) 40
    (B) 80
    (C) 160
    (D) 320
    (E) 640

Coordinate Plane

❑ The **coordinate plane** is a grid made up of two number lines – a horizontal number line called the **x-axis** and a vertical number line called the **y-axis**. These two lines meet at a point called the **origin**. This is the point where both number lines are labeled zero.

The *x*-axis is used to measure the value of *x* at any point on the plane. Points to the right of the origin have positive values of *x*, and points to the left of the origin have negative values of *x*.

The *y*-axis is used to measure the value of *y* at any point on the plane. Points above the origin have positive values of *y*, and points below the origin have negative values of *y*.

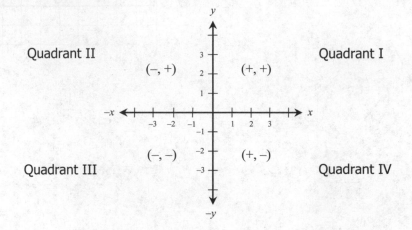

❑ We can describe the position of a point on the plane using a pair of numbers called an **ordered pair**. An ordered pair is also called the **coordinates** of the point.

The first number in the pair is the value of *x* at the point, called the **x-coordinate**.

The second number in the pair is the value of *y* at the point, called the **y-coordinate**.

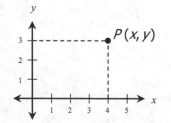

In the figure above, *P* has coordinates $(4, 3)$.

TRY IT OUT

1. Plot the following points on the graph below:

   A: (2, 2)   B: (−5, −1)   C: (4, −2)

   D: (−5, 3)   E: (−4, −3)   F: (−2, 4)

2. Find the coordinates of the following points:

   K:____   L:____   M:____

   N:____   P:____

   Q:____   R:____   S:____

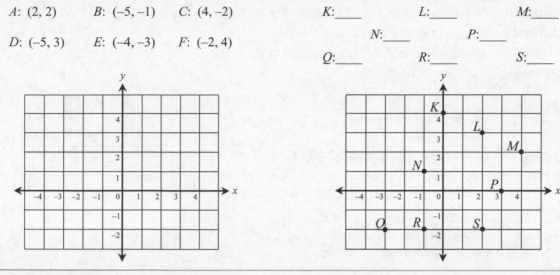

PUT IT TOGETHER

1. In the coordinate plane, point (2, 1) lies on the circumference of a circle with a radius of 3 units. Which of the following points could NOT lie on the circumference of the circle?

   (A) (5, 1)
   (B) (8, 1)
   (C) (2, −5)
   (D) (−4, 1)
   (E) (2, 7)

2.

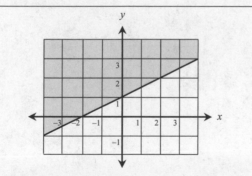

The graph of the inequality $2y \geq x + 2$ is shown in the *xy*-coordinate plane. If point Z is NOT contained within the shaded region, which of the following could be the coordinates of Z?

   (A) (0, 1)
   (B) (1, 2)
   (C) (−3, 1)
   (D) (−3, −1)
   (E) (−4, −1)

Midpoint & Distance

❑ The **midpoint** of a line segment is the point exactly in the middle between two end points. To find the midpoint, calculate the average of the *x*-coordinates and the average of the *y*-coordinates.

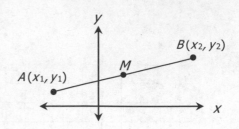

Midpoint $= \left(\dfrac{x_1 + x_2}{2}, \dfrac{y_1 + y_2}{2} \right)$, where (x_1, y_1) and (x_2, y_2) are the endpoints of the line segment.

❑ Distance between points (x_1, y_1) and (x_2, y_2), =

$$\sqrt{(x_2 - x_1)^2 + (y_2 - y_1)^2}$$

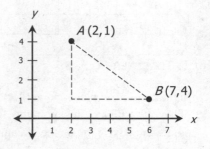

This equation is based on the Pythagorean Theorem. You can draw intersecting vertical and horizontal lines from the two given points on a line to create a right triangle, with the distance between the two points as the hypotenuse, and then simply use the Pythagorean Theorem to solve for the distance between the two points.

What is the distance between $(2, 2)$ and $(-2, -1)$?

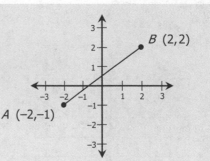

Use the distance formula to solve:

Now solve by plotting points and drawing a right triangle:

TRY IT OUT

Use the graph below to answer the following questions:

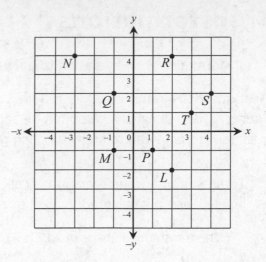

1. What is the midpoint of the line segment *PT*?

2. What is the midpoint of the line segment *MS*?

3. What is the distance between points *N* and *Q*?

4. What is the distance between points *N* and *L*?

PUT IT TOGETHER

1.

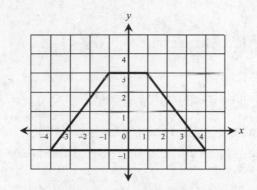

What is the perimeter, in units, of quadrilateral shown in the *xy*-coordinate grid above?

(A) 14
(B) 15
(C) 18
(D) 20
(E) 30

---

2. Claire lives 5 miles north from school, and Yuki lives 12 miles west from the same school. In miles, how far is Claire's house from Yuki's house?

(A) 7
(B) 11
(C) 13
(D) 17
(E) Cannot be determined from the information given

Transformations

A transformation is an alteration to a figure.

Most questions in this category require carefully mapping changes to coordinate points or figures. These questions can often be solved by visualizing the transformations. Occasionally, questions require you to know function graph transformation rules.

❑ The result of a transformation is called the "image" of the original figure. The image is often labeled with a small mark (called a "prime").

The transformed image of *XYZ* is *X'Y'Z'*.

❑ **Translation** is the process of moving a point or figure a specified distance in a certain direction.

If $P(-1, 1)$ is shifted down 3 units, what will be the coordinates of P'? _____

❑ **Reflection** is the process of moving a point or figure by mirroring it over a line.

A helpful way to visualize a reflection is to imagine the ink on the figure is wet, then fold the paper along the reflecting line. The imprint of the figure on the other side of the line is the reflection.

If $P(-1, 1)$ is reflected over the *y*-axis, what will be the coordinates of P'? _____

❑ **Rotation** is the process of moving a point or figure by rotating it around a point – often the origin.

The best way to visualize rotation is to draw a line segment from a point on the figure to the origin (or whatever point the figure is rotated around). Then, keeping the end on the origin fixed, rotate the line by the specified amount (like the minute hand on a clock). The endpoint of the rotated line is the new rotated point.

If $P(-1, 1)$ is rotated 180° about the origin, what will be the coordinates of P'? _____

❑ Shapes have **symmetry** when they can be transformed to be exactly like one another. An axis of symmetry is a line that divides a figure into symmetrical images.

PUT IT TOGETHER

1.

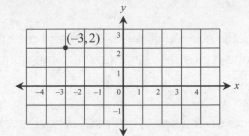

The point shown in the diagram above is translated right 6 units and up 1 unit. What are the coordinates of the point after these transformations?

(A) (3,2)
(B) (3,3)
(C) (–2,–4)
(D) (–2,8)
(E) (–4,8)

2. Point M (2,2) is translated 3 units left then reflected over the y-axis onto point M'. What are the coordinates of M''?

(A) (–5,2)
(B) (–1,–2)
(C) (1,2)
(D) (1,5)
(E) (5,–2)

3.

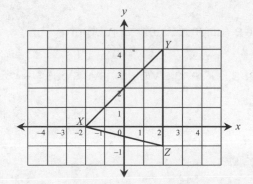

The triangle XYZ, shown in the diagram above, is rotated 90° clockwise about the origin and then translated 3 units up onto triangle $X'Y'Z'$. What are the coordinates of Y'?

(A) (–4,2)
(B) (–7,2)
(C) (–4,5)
(D) (4,1)
(E) (7,–2)

Slope

❑ The **slope** is the amount a line moves vertically for every unit the line moves horizontally. Lines that slant up to the right have positive slope. Lines that slant down to the right have negative slope.

❑ Use $\dfrac{\textbf{rise}}{\textbf{run}}$ to calculate slope. First, find two points on the line. The "rise" is how much the y value increases. The "run" is how much the x value increases between two points. The ratio of rise to run is the slope of the line through those points.

In other words, the slope of a line that passes through points (x_1, y_1) and (x_2, y_2) is given by the formula: $\textbf{slope} = \dfrac{(\textbf{\textit{y}}_2 - \textbf{\textit{y}}_1)}{(\textbf{\textit{x}}_2 - \textbf{\textit{x}}_1)}$

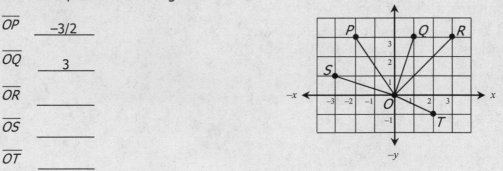

Find the slopes of the line segments:

$\overline{OP}$ ___−3/2___

$\overline{OQ}$ ___3___

$\overline{OR}$ _____

$\overline{OS}$ _____

$\overline{OT}$ _____

❑ The slopes of **perpendicular lines** are negative reciprocals of each other.

For a line with slope $\dfrac{a}{b}$, a line that crosses it at a 90° angle would have slope $\dfrac{-b}{a}$.

❑ **Parallel lines** have equal slopes.

❑ **Vertical lines** have undefined slope, or infinite slope.

❑ **Horizontal lines** have slope = 0.

TRY IT OUT

Use the graph below to answer the following questions:

1. What is the slope of the line through points T and S?

2. What is the slope of the line through points L and T?

3. What is the slope of the line through points R and T?

4. What is the slope of the line through points Q and R?

5. What is the slope of the line through points M and L?

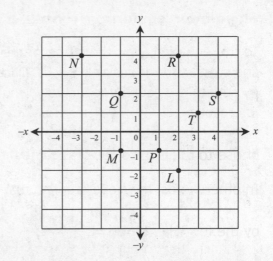

6. The line between L and what point has a slope of 2?

7. The line between N and what point has a slope of $-\dfrac{1}{2}$?

PUT IT TOGETHER

1. A line with slope -3 passes through the points $(p, 8)$ and $(6, -1)$ in the xy-coordinate plane. What is the value of p?

    (A) -19
    (B) 0
    (C) 3
    (D) 9
    (E) 15

2. In the xy-coordinate plane, what is the slope of a line perpendicular to the line with equation $2x + 6y = 3$?

    (A) 3

    (B) 2

    (C) $\dfrac{3}{2}$

    (D) $\dfrac{1}{2}$

    (E) $\dfrac{1}{3}$

Graphing Lines

❑ **Slope-intercept form**: $y = mx + b$.

In this equation, **m** is the **slope** of the line and **b** is the **y-intercept** (the point where the line crosses the y-axis and $x = 0$). Once you have converted a line to slope-intercept form, by setting the equation equal to y, you can easily identify the slope of the line and its y-intercept.

> If a line is given by the equation $6x - 2y = 7$, what are the slope and y-intercept of the line?
>
> 1. Put the equation in slope-intercept form by setting it equal to y.
>
> $$6x - 2y = 7 \quad \Rightarrow \quad -2y = -6x + 7 \quad \Rightarrow \quad y = 3x - \frac{7}{2}$$
>
> 2. For the equation $y = mx + b$, the slope is m and the y-intercept is b.
>
> $$\text{slope} = 3 \qquad y\text{-intercept} = -\frac{7}{2}$$

❑ To graph the equation of a line in slope-intercept form, you can begin with the y-intercept and then draw a line with the equation's slope from that point.

You can also input values of x and find corresponding values of y, then plot the coordinates, and then connect the points to create a line.

> Graph the equation $y = \frac{1}{2}x + 1$:
>
>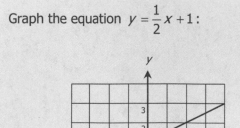
>
> y-intercept = 1
>
> slope = $\frac{1}{2}$
>
> $$x = 0 \quad \Rightarrow \quad y = \frac{1}{2}(0) + 1 \quad \Rightarrow \quad y = 1$$
>
> So, when $x = 0$, $y = 1$.
>
> $$x = 4 \quad \Rightarrow \quad y = \frac{1}{2}(4) + 1 \quad \Rightarrow \quad y = 3$$
>
> So, when $x = 4$, $y = 3$

TRY IT OUT

1. Graph the following line equations:

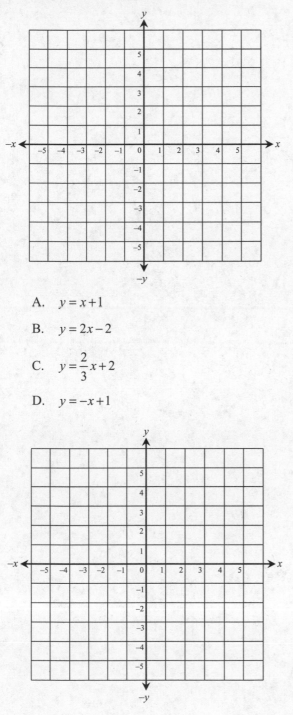

A. $y = x + 1$

B. $y = 2x - 2$

C. $y = \dfrac{2}{3}x + 2$

D. $y = -x + 1$

E. $y = -2x - 2$

F. $2y - x = 2$

G. $x = 3$

H. $y = -4$

2. Find the equations for the lines in the graph below:

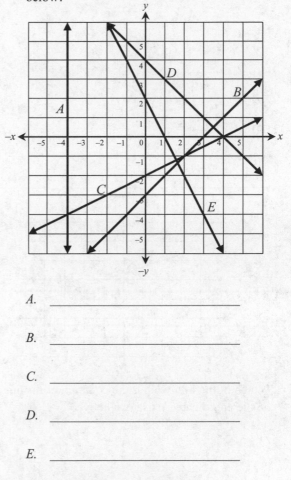

A. _____

B. _____

C. _____

D. _____

E. _____

3. Write the equation of a line with a slope of 1 that passes through the point $(-3, 1)$.

4. Write the equation of a line with a slope of -3 that passes through the point $(2, -4)$.

5. Write the equation of the line that passes through the points $(-3, 1)$ and $(6, -5)$.

PUT IT TOGETHER

1. Which equation represents a line parallel to the graph of
    $x + 2y = 4$ on the xy-coordinate plane?

    (A) $y = \dfrac{1}{2}x + 4$

    (B) $y = -\dfrac{1}{2}x + 4$

    (C) $y = -2x + 4$

    (D) $y = 2x + 4$

    (E) $y = 4x + 4$

2.

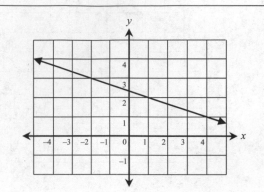

    Which of the following is the equation of the line graphed
    on the coordinate grid shown above?

    (A) $y = -\dfrac{1}{3}x + 2\dfrac{1}{3}$

    (B) $y = -\dfrac{1}{3}x + 2\dfrac{2}{3}$

    (C) $y = \dfrac{1}{3}x + 2\dfrac{1}{3}$

    (D) $y = 3x + 2\dfrac{1}{2}$

    (E) $y = 3x + 2\dfrac{2}{3}$

3. Which of the following graphs represents a linear function?

(A)

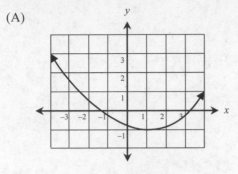

(B)

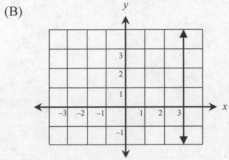

(C)

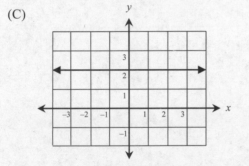

(D)

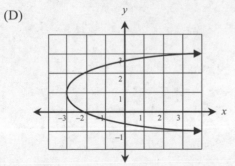

(E)

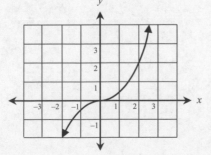

Checkpoint Review

1. The figure shows the location of Anna's office and her house. Each grid mark represents 1 mile.

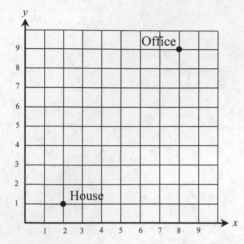

What is the distance, in miles, between Anna's office and her house?

(A) 2
(B) 10
(C) 12
(D) 14
(E) 20

2. Brenda lives 4 kilometers from a train station. Han lives 7 miles from the same train station. How far, in kilometers, is Brenda's house from Han's house?

(A) 3
(B) 5.5
(C) 8
(D) 11
(E) Cannot be determined from the information given

Checkpoint Review

3. The point P $(-2,-3)$ is reflected across the x-axis then rotated 180° counter-clockwise about the origin onto point P'. What are the coordinates of point P''?

    (A) $(-2,-3)$
    (B) $(2,3)$
    (C) $(2,-3)$
    (D) $(-3,-2)$
    (E) $(-3,2)$

---

4. The trapezoid $RSTU$ is translated 3 units down and then reflected over the x-axis onto $R'S'T'U'$. What are the coordinates of S'?

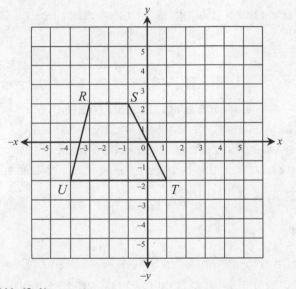

    (A) $(2,1)$
    (B) $(2,-1)$
    (C) $(1,1)$
    (D) $(1,-1)$
    (E) $(-1,1)$

Chapter Review

❑ Angles

A 90° angle is called a right angle. The measure of a straight line is equal to 180°. Guesstimate angles on figures that are drawn to scale.

❑ Parallel Lines

When two lines intersect, the angles opposite each other are called vertical angles. Vertical angles are equal.

❑ Isosceles and Equilateral Triangles

An isosceles triangle is any triangle that has two equal sides. In addition, the angles opposite the congruent sides are equal. An equilateral triangle is a triangle that has all three sides equal. In addition, all angles are 60°.

❑ Right Triangles

A right triangle is any triangle that has a 90° angle as one of its angles. The two sides that form the right angle are the legs. The third side is the hypotenuse. The hypotenuse is opposite the right angle, and it is the longest side of a right triangle. The Pythagorean Theorem states that in any right triangle the square of the hypotenuse is equal to the sum of the squares of the other two sides.

❑ Area and Perimeter – Rectangle and Square

Perimeter is the distance around the edge of a two-dimensional figure. Area is the measurement of the space inside a two-dimensional figure. Area is measured in square units. A rectangle is a 4-sided figure with 4 right angles. In a rectangle, opposite sides are equal. A square is a rectangle that has 4 equal sides.

❑ Area and Perimeter – Triangle

To find the perimeter of a triangle, add the lengths of all of the sides. To find the area of a triangle, use the following formula: $A = \dfrac{1}{2}bh$, where A = area, b = base, and h = height.

❑ Circles

Circumference is the distance around the edge of the circle. Circumference = $2 \times \pi \times r$

The area of a circle is found using the formula: Area = $\pi \times r^2$

❑ Volume

Volume is the space occupied by a three-dimensional figure. Volume of a cube: $V = s^3$
Volume of a rectangular box: $V = l \times w \times h$

❑ Spatial Reasoning

Spatial reasoning questions test your problem-solving skills and your ability to visualize 2-dimensional and 3-dimensional situations. During the test, use anything available to help solve spatial reasoning questions.

❑ Midpoint & Distance

The midpoint of a line segment is the point exactly in the middle between two end points. To find the midpoint, calculate the average of the x-coordinates and the average of the y-coordinates.

Distance between points (x_1, y_1) and $(x_2, y_2),$ = $\sqrt{(x_2 - x_1)^2 + (y_2 - y_1)^2}$

❑ Transformations

Translation is the process of moving a point or figure a specified distance in a certain direction. Reflection is the process of moving a point or figure by mirroring it over a line. Rotation is the process of moving a point or figure by rotating it around a point – often the origin. Shapes have symmetry when they can be transformed to be exactly like one another. An axis of symmetry is a line that divides a figure into symmetrical images.

❑ Slope

The slope is the amount a line moves vertically for every unit the line moves horizontally.

Use $\dfrac{\text{rise}}{\text{run}}$ to calculate slope. The slopes of perpendicular lines are negative reciprocals of each other. Parallel lines have equal slopes. Vertical lines have undefined slope, or infinite slope. Horizontal lines have slope = 0.

❑ Graphing Lines

Slope-intercept form: $y = mx + b$. In this equation, m is the slope of the line and b is the y-intercept (the point where the line crosses the y-axis and $x = 0$).

Geometry Practice

Angles

1.

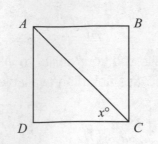

If *ABCD* is a square, what is the value of *x*?

(A) 30
(B) 45
(C) 60
(D) 90
(E) It cannot be determined from the information given.

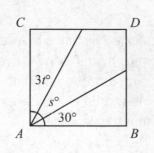

2. In the figure above, *ABCD* is a square. What is the value of $2(3t + s)$?

(A) 30°
(B) 60°
(C) 90°
(D) 120°
(E) It cannot be determined from the information given.

---

3. If the angle measures of a triangle are represented by $2x°$, $3x°$, and $4x°$, what is the value of *x*?

(A) 10
(B) 20
(C) 30
(D) 40
(E) It cannot be determined from the information given.

Parallel Lines

4. In the figure shown below, line a is parallel to line b.
    What is the value of x?

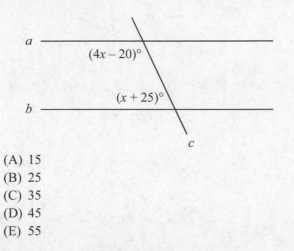

(A) 15
(B) 25
(C) 35
(D) 45
(E) 55

Isosceles and Equilateral Triangles

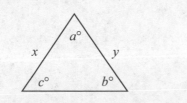

5. What is the perimeter of triangle ABC shown above?

(A) $x + y$
(B) $x + 2y$
(C) $2x + y$
(D) $3x - y$
(E) $3x$

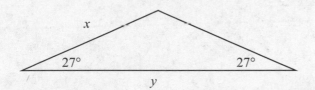

6. In the figure shown above, if $x = y$ and $a = b$, what is the
    value of c?

(A) 15
(B) 30
(C) 45
(D) 60
(E) 90

Right Triangles

7. A 24-foot tall telephone pole is reinforced by a cable that is secured in the ground 18 feet from the base of the pole.

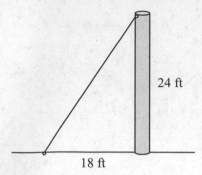

    What is the length of the cable?

    (A) 30 feet
    (B) 32 feet
    (C) 36 feet
    (D) 40 feet
    (E) 42 feet

Area and Perimeter

8. A rectangle has side lengths of x and $x + 3$. If the perimeter of the rectangle is 30, then what is the length of the longer side?

    (A) 3
    (B) 6
    (C) 9
    (D) 12
    (E) 27

9.

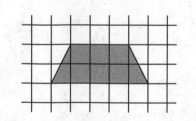

    In the figure shown above, lines are spaced 1 unit apart. What is the area, in square units, of the shaded figure?

    (A) 16
    (B) 17
    (C) 8
    (D) 7
    (E) 6

Circles

10.

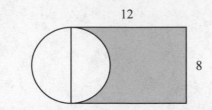

Find the area of the shaded region in the figure above in square units. Use the value 3.14 for π.

(A) 4.48
(B) 45.76
(C) 70.88
(D) 83.44
(E) 89.72

11.

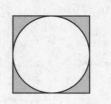

In the figure above, a circle is inscribed in a square. If the circumference of the circle is 16π, what is the perimeter of the square?

(A) 16
(B) 32
(C) 64
(D) 128
(E) 256

Volume

12.

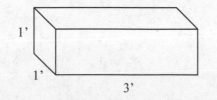

How many 1" × 1" × 1" blocks can be formed from the rectangular block above?

(A) 5,184
(B) 3,000
(C) 1,728
(D) 576
(E) 3

Spatial Reasoning

13. Which of the following shapes can be made by putting two triangles together without overlapping?

    I.   Rectangle
    II. Square
    III. Triangle

    (A) I only
    (B) II only
    (C) I and II only
    (D) I, II, and III
    (E) None of the above

14.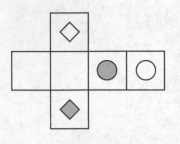

The net of a cube is shown above. Which of the following could be an image of three adjacent sides of the cube?

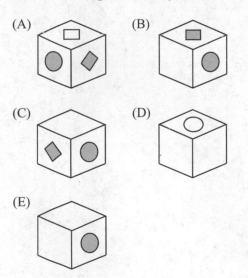

(A)

(B)

(C)

(D)

(E)

15. If a plane intersects with a cone, which of the following could NOT be the cross-section of the cone?

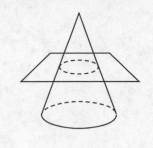

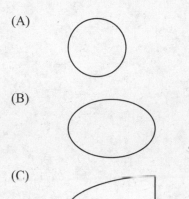

(A)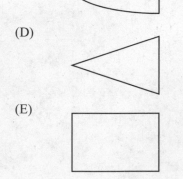

(B)

(C)

(D)

(E)

Coordinate Plane

16.

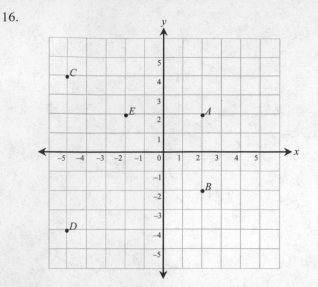

In the graph shown above, which point has the coordinates $(-2, 2)$?

(A) A
(B) B
(C) C
(D) D
(E) E

---

17. On the xy-coordinate plane, $\triangle ABC$ is formed by the points with the following coordinates:

$A\,(-1, 4)$, $B\,(-1, -2)$, $C\,(2, 4)$.

What is the area of $\triangle ABC$?

(A) 3
(B) 6
(C) 9
(D) 18
(E) 27

Midpoint and Distance

18. Ari hikes 3 miles east and then 5 miles north to a camp site. What is the shortest distance, in miles, from the camp site to Ari's starting point?

    (A) $\sqrt{34}$
    (B) $\sqrt{24}$
    (C) $\sqrt{16}$
    (D) $\sqrt{8}$
    (E) $\sqrt{4}$

Transformations

19. A pentagon is in the fourth quadrant of the coordinate plane, as shown below.

    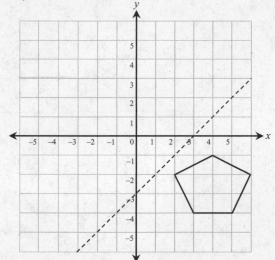

    How many vertices of the pentagon will be in the fourth quadrant after it is reflected over the dotted line?

    (A) 1
    (B) 2
    (C) 3
    (D) 4
    (E) 5

20. If point K is at $(9, 3)$ in the coordinate plane, what is the new position of point K after it is rotated 270° clockwise about the origin?

    (A) $(-9, -3)$
    (B) $(-9, 3)$
    (C) $(9, -3)$
    (D) $(3, -9)$
    (E) $(-3, 9)$

Slope

21. The slope of the line $3x - 2y = 12$ is

    (A) -6

    (B) $-\dfrac{2}{3}$

    (C) $\dfrac{2}{3}$

    (D) $\dfrac{3}{2}$

    (E) 4

22. What is the slope of the line through points $(-3, 2)$ and $(5, -4)$?

    (A) $-\dfrac{4}{3}$

    (B) $-\dfrac{3}{4}$

    (C) $\dfrac{3}{4}$

    (D) $\dfrac{4}{3}$

    (E) $\dfrac{1}{2}$

Graphing Lines

23.

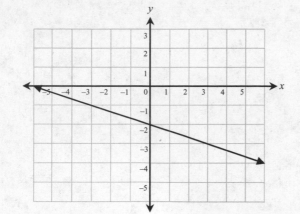

What is the equation of the graphed line shown above?

(A) $y = -3x - 2$

(B) $y = -2x - \dfrac{1}{3}$

(C) $y = 2x + \dfrac{1}{3}$

(D) $y = -\dfrac{1}{3}x - 3$

(E) $y = -\dfrac{1}{3}x - 2$

---

24. What is the y-intercept of $2y + 8x - 6 = 0$ when graphed on the xy-coordinate plane?

(A) -4

(B) $\dfrac{3}{4}$

(C) $\dfrac{4}{3}$

(D) 3

(E) 4

---

25. A line on the coordinate plane passes through points $(2, 1)$ and $(-2, -3)$. Which of the following is the equation of the line?

(A) $y = 2x$
(B) $y = x + 1$
(C) $y = x - 1$
(D) $y = -x + 1$
(E) $y = -x - 1$

Geometry Practice – Middle Level

1.

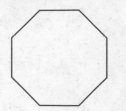

The figure above shows a polygon with sides of equal length. If the perimeter of the polygon is 160, what is the length of each side?

(A) 2
(B) 10
(C) 18
(D) 20
(E) 22

2. Which of the following coordinates represents a point located in the fourth quadrant of the xy-coordinate plane?

(A) (2, 1)
(B) (–1, 2)
(C) (–1, –2)
(D) (–2, –1)
(E) (1, –2)

3.

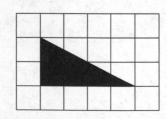

In the figure shown above, what is the area of the shaded region if the area of each square is 1?

(A) 4
(B) 8
(C) 16
(D) 24
(E) It cannot be determined from the information given.

4.

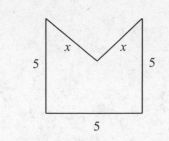

If the perimeter of the figure above is 21, the value of x is

(A) 9
(B) 4
(C) 3
(D) 2
(E) 1

5. If a square is folded in half, which of the following could result?

I.   A square
II. A triangle
III. A rectangle

(A) None
(B) III only
(C) I and III only
(D) II and III only
(E) I, II, and III

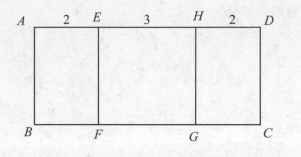

6. In the figure shown above, what is the area of $ABCD$ if $EFGH$ is a square?

(A) 14
(B) 20
(C) 21
(D) 36
(E) It cannot be determined from the information given.

7.

If the rectangle above is folded in half along the dotted line, which of the following figures could be the result?

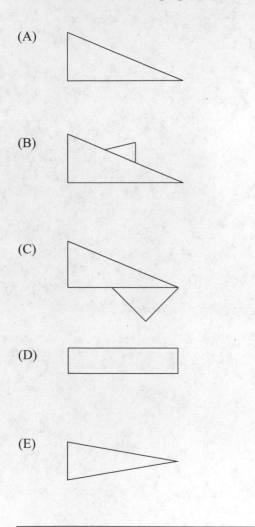

(A)

(B)

(C)

(D)

(E)

8. Kenny uses 4 gallons of paint to paint a rectangular ceiling 20 feet wide by 50 feet long. How many gallons of paint does he use per square foot?

(A) .004
(B) .04
(C) .4
(D) 1
(E) 4

9. If a rectangle has an area of 16, then what pair could NOT be the length and width of the rectangle?

(A) 2, 8
(B) 4, 4
(C) 1, 7
(D) 1, 16
(E) $\frac{1}{2}$, 32

10.

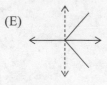

In the figure shown, what is the value of x?

(A) 45
(B) 55
(C) 65
(D) 145
(E) 155

11. Which graph, if folded along the dotted line, would overlap exactly?

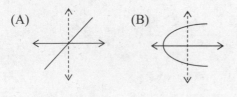

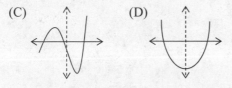

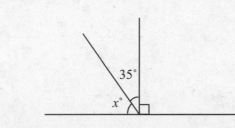

12. What is the average length of a side of a quadrilateral that has a perimeter of 48?

(A) 6
(B) 8
(C) 12
(D) 208
(E) It cannot be determined from the information given.

---

13. A square has a side length of 7. What is the difference between its area and its perimeter?

(A) 7
(B) 14
(C) 21
(D) 28
(E) 49

---

14. How many circles of diameter 3' can be placed in a 12' × 7' rectangle, if none of the circles overlap each other?

(A) 4
(B) 6
(C) 7
(D) 8
(E) 12

---

15. As shown in the figure, ABCD is a square.

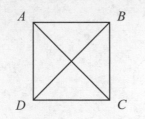

What path is the longest?

(A) A to B to C to D
(B) A to D to B to C
(C) A to B to D to C
(D) A to C to B to D
(E) A to B to C to A

16. A certain triangle has different angle measures for each angle. Which of the following MUST be a classification of the triangle?

(A) Equilateral
(B) Isosceles
(C) Right
(D) Obtuse
(E) Scalene

17.

Note: Figure not drawn to scale.

A pyramid with four sides rests on a flat surface, as shown in the figure above. If the part of the pyramid touching the flat, circular surface was dipped in black ink before touching the surface, which of the following could be a representation of what the flat surface would look like if the pyramid were removed?

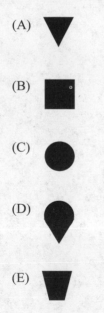

(A)

(B)

(C)

(D)

(E)

18.

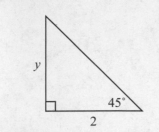

What is the value of *y* in the figure above?

(A) 2

(B) $2\sqrt{2}$

(C) $2\sqrt{3}$

(D) 4

(E) It cannot be determined from the information given.

19. 90 unit cubes will exactly fill a certain rectangular prism. If the width of the prism is 3 units and the length is twice the width, what is the prism's height, in units?

(A) 20

(B) 15

(C) 10

(D) 5

(E) 2.5

20. Hap drew a line segment with one endpoint in the first quadrant and the other endpoint in the fourth quadrant. Which of the following could NOT be the slope of the line segment?

(A) –2

(B) $-\dfrac{1}{2}$

(C) 0

(D) $\dfrac{1}{2}$

(E) 2

21. How many squares 2 inches on a side can be cut from a piece of paper 10 inches wide by 12 inches long?

(A) 4

(B) 20

(C) 30

(D) 60

(E) 120

22. *MR*, *NQ*, and *OP* are line segments that intersect at point *S*. The measure of angle *MSN* is 49° and angle *PSR* is 85°.

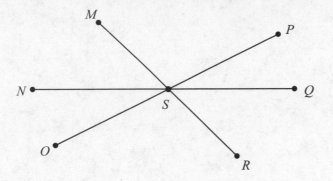

What is the measure of angle *PSQ*?

(A) 14°
(B) 36°
(C) 46°
(D) 56°
(E) 95°

23.

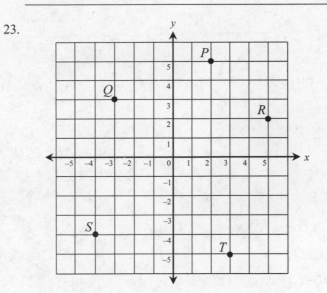

Points *P*, *Q*, *R*, *S*, *T* are shown in the *xy*-coordinate grid.
Which of the following is the same distance as *PS*?

(A) *PT*
(B) *PQ*
(C) *RS*
(D) *RT*
(E) *QT*

24.

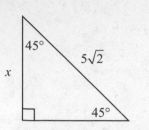

What does *x* equal in the figure above?

(A) 4
(B) $4\sqrt{2}$
(C) 5
(D) 10
(E) It cannot be determined from the information given.

25. Raj placed a paper triangle in the *xy*-coordinate plane.

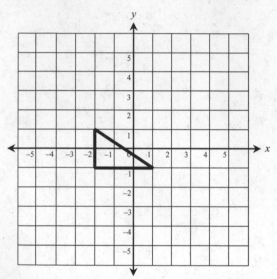

Which of the following transformations can Raj apply to the triangle so all of its vertices are in the second quadrant?

(A) a translation 2 units left and 5 units up
(B) a translation 2 units left and 2 units down
(C) a translation 3 units right and 3 units up
(D) a translation 3 units right and 4 units down
(E) a translation 2 units right and 1 unit down

Geometry Practice – Upper Level

1.

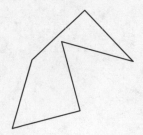

All of the sides of the shape shown in the figure above have a length of 6. What is the perimeter?

(A) 1
(B) 6
(C) 12
(D) 36
(E) It cannot be determined from the information given.

---

2. A square has a perimeter of 16x. What is the length of a side of the square?

(A) 2
(B) 4
(C) 8
(D) 2x
(E) 4x

---

3. A prison is surrounded by 11 sides. If the perimeter of the prison is 220 yards, what is the average length in <u>feet</u> of one of the sides?

(A) 20
(B) 30
(C) 60
(D) 66
(E) 204

4. The figure shows a map of several streets which form two squares where they intersect (shaded).

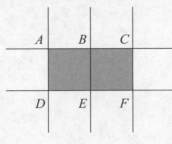

If the distance from *A* to *B* is 2 miles, which of the following routes from *A* to *F* is 6 miles long?

(A) *A* to *B* to *C* to *D* to *E* to *F*
(B) *A* to *E* to *C* to *F*
(C) *A* to *D* to *B* to *F*
(D) *A* to *B* to *E* to *F*
(E) None of the above

5.

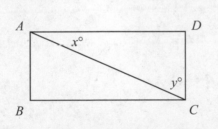

If *ABCD* is a rectangle, what is *y* in terms of *x*?

(A) x
(B) $90 - x$
(C) $90 + x$
(D) $180 - x$
(E) $360 - x$

6. 24 feet of fence enclose Dan's rectangular back yard.

What is the length of Dan's yard, if the width is $\frac{1}{3}$ of the length?

(A) 3 feet
(B) 6 feet
(C) 9 feet
(D) 18 feet
(E) 64 feet

SUMMIT
EDUCATIONAL
GROUP

7. 20 squares, each measuring three inches on a side, can be cut from a piece of cloth with no cloth left over. What is the area of the cloth in square inches?

   (A) 9
   (B) 60
   (C) 180
   (D) 200
   (E) 1,800

8.

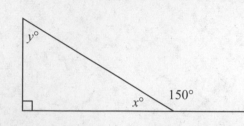

In the figure above, $y =$

   (A) 30
   (B) 40
   (C) 45
   (D) 50
   (E) 60

9.

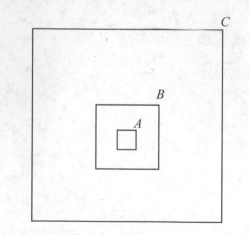

In the figure above, A, B, and C are squares. The area of C is 9 times that of B. The area of B is 9 times that of A. What is the ratio of the length of a side of A to the length of a side of C?

   (A) 1 to 3
   (B) 1 to 9
   (C) 9 to 1
   (D) 18 to 1
   (E) 1 to 27

10.

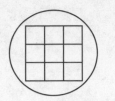

9 four inch by four inch brownies are arranged on a circular tray as shown in the figure above. Which of the following could be the diameter of the tray?

(A) 3 inches
(B) 4 inches
(C) 9 inches
(D) 12 inches
(E) 18 inches

11.

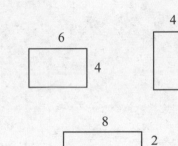

The rectangles shown in the figure above are repositioned without any overlapping so that the result is a square. Which of the following is the area of that square?

(A) 16
(B) 36
(C) 64
(D) 96
(E) 144

12.

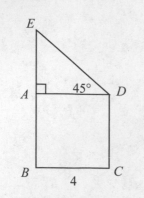

In the figure above, *ABCD* is a square with side of length 4. What is the area of polygon *ABCDE*?

(A) 16
(B) 24
(C) 30
(D) 36
(E) 48

---

13. In the figure shown below, what is the length, in inches, of the missing side?

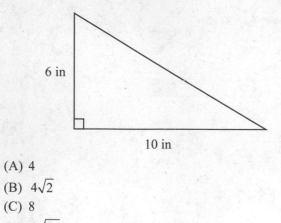

6 in

10 in

(A) 4
(B) $4\sqrt{2}$
(C) 8
(D) $2\sqrt{34}$
(E) 14

14. In the figure shown below, segment *l* is parallel to segment *m*. What is the value of *x*?

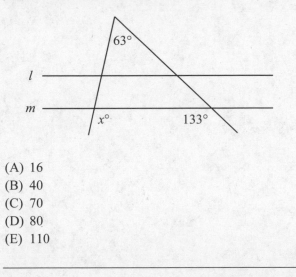

(A) 16
(B) 40
(C) 70
(D) 80
(E) 110

15. There are two circular paths around a park. The inner path has a radius of 1,000 feet and the outer path has a radius of 1,500 feet. What is the difference in distance between the two paths?

(A) 500 feet
(B) 1,000 feet
(C) 500π feet
(D) 2,500 feet
(E) 1,000π feet

16. In the figure shown below, what is the value of *x*?

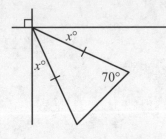

(A) 10
(B) 15
(C) 20
(D) 25
(E) 30

17. What is the measure of each angle in a regular hexagon?

(A) 45

(B) 75

(C) 105

(D) 120

(E) 150

18. Triangle *ABC* is similar to triangle *ADE*.

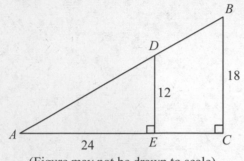

(Figure may not be drawn to scale)

What is the length, in units, of *AC*?

(A) 12

(B) 16

(C) 20

(D) 36

(E) 60

19. What is the value of *x*?

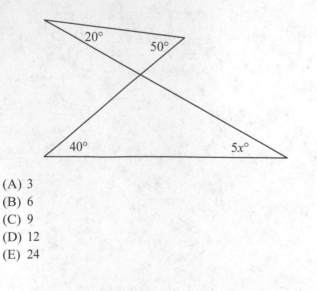

(A) 3

(B) 6

(C) 9

(D) 12

(E) 24

20. What is the circumference, in terms of π, of a circle with area 49π ft^2?

    (A) 7π ft
    (B) 14π ft
    (C) 28π ft
    (D) 49π ft
    (E) 98π ft

21. In the standard (x, y) coordinate plane, which of the following is the equation of a line parallel to $y = x + 2$ that includes the point $(3, -1)$?

    (A) $y = -x + 2$
    (B) $y = x - 4$
    (C) $y = x - 3$
    (D) $y = x + 2$
    (E) $y = x + 4$

22. In the xy-coordinate plane, the graph of $x - 3y = 4$ intersects the y-axis at point P. What are the coordinates of P?

    (A) $-\dfrac{4}{3}$

    (B) $-\dfrac{3}{4}$

    (C) $\dfrac{3}{4}$

    (D) $\dfrac{4}{3}$

    (E) 4

23. The width of rectangle X is half the width of rectangle Y.

    The length of rectangle X is $\dfrac{3}{2}$ the length of rectangle Y.

    If the area of rectangle Y is n times the area of rectangle X, what is the value of n?

    (A) $\dfrac{1}{3}$

    (B) $\dfrac{2}{3}$

    (C) $\dfrac{3}{4}$

    (D) $\dfrac{4}{3}$

    (E) 3

24. How many quadrilaterals are shown in the figure below?

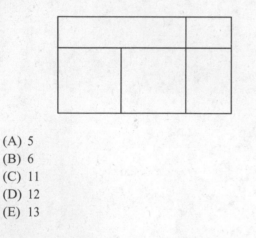

    (A) 5
    (B) 6
    (C) 11
    (D) 12
    (E) 13

25. An equilateral triangle has side lengths of 8 units. What is the area, in square units, of the triangle?

    (A) $32\sqrt{3}$
    (B) $16\sqrt{3}$
    (C) $8\sqrt{3}$
    (D) $4\sqrt{3}$
    (E) $2\sqrt{3}$

Data Analysis & Probability

❑ Averages   294

❑ Median, Mode, & Range   298

❑ Sets   300

❑ Counting   302

❑ Probability   304

❑ Interpreting Data   308

Averages

❑ To find the average of a list of numbers, find the sum of the numbers and divide by the number of terms.

$$\textbf{Average} = \frac{\text{sum of parts}}{\text{number of parts}}$$

> Joanne's test scores were 73, 90, 82, 85, and 80. What was her average test score?
>
> $$\frac{73 + 90 + 82 + 85 + 80}{5} = \frac{410}{5} = 82$$

❑ **ANT** – **A**verage x **N**umber = **T**otal – To solve some SSAT average problems, you need to use this formula in reverse, solving for the sum when you are given the average.

(average) × (number of parts) = sum of parts

> The average weight of a group of 10 men is 150 lbs. One of these men weighs 200 lbs. What is the average weight of the other men?
>
> First, find the total weight of the group: $10 \times 150 = 1,500$
>
> Now, find the total weight for the other 9 men: $1,500 - 200 = 1,300$
>
> Now, find the average: $\frac{1,300}{9} = 144.44$ lbs.

❑ **Never Average Two Averages** – To find the average of two averages, you must first find the two subtotals, add them, and then divide by the combined number of parts.

TRY IT OUT

1. What is the average of 12 and 20?

2. What is the average of 50, 100, and 150?

3. John is 12 years old, Sarah is 10 years old, Mark is 8 years old, and Tom is 6 years old. What is the average age of the 4 children?

4. The Minnesota Wild hockey team won 25 games the first season, 42 games the second season, and 50 games the third season. What is the average number of games won by the Minnesota Wild over those three seasons?

5. Karen sold 5 chocolate bars on Monday, 9 chocolate bars on Tuesday, 4 chocolate bars on Wednesday, none on Thursday, and 7 chocolate bars on Friday. What is the average number of chocolate bars Karen sold each day?

6. A basketball player averages 20 points per game for the first 8 games. After 9 games, his average is 18 points per game. How many points did he score in the ninth game?

7. Jill scores an average of 3 runs per game for the first 10 games of the softball season. After 12 games, her average is 4 runs per game. How many runs did she score in the last two games?

8. Michael's average grade for 7 math tests is 92. After the eighth test his average is 87. What was his grade on the eighth math test?

9. After working for 6 weeks, Susan's average weekly salary is $160. For the first 3 weeks her average salary was $150. What was her average weekly salary for the last 3 weeks?

10. The average age of a group of 7 children is 10. If the youngest child is 3, and the oldest child is 12, what is the average age of the other 5 children?

PUT IT TOGETHER

1. The table below shows the number of customers who visited a souvenir shop over a week.

Day	Sun	Mon	Tue	Wed	Thu	Fri	Sat
Customer	27	14	11	9	16	20	29

    What was the mean number of daily customers for the week?

    (A) 17
    (B) 18
    (C) 19
    (D) 20
    (E) 21

2. The average age of two girls is 19 and the average age of three boys is 9. What is the average age of all five people?

    (A) 16
    (B) 15
    (C) 14
    (D) 13
    (E) 12

3.   {21, 13, 40, 19, 7, 14}

    For the data set shown above, which number, if added to the set, would not change the set's mean?

    (A) 14
    (B) 16
    (C) 19
    (D) 24
    (E) 29

4. Which of the following <u>must</u> be true of the numbers m and n if m is greater than n and the two numbers have an average of 100?

(A) $100 - m = 100$
(B) $m = 100 - n$
(C) $m = 100 + n$
(D) $m - n = 50$
(E) $m + n = 200$

Median, Mode, & Range

❑ The **median** of a set of numbers is the middle value when all the terms are listed in order according to size.

When there is an odd number of terms, the median is one of the terms in the set. When there is an even number of terms in the set, the median is the mean of the middle two terms.

> In the set {2, 15, 11, 7, 5, 15, 52}, 11 is the median.

❑ The **mode** of a set of numbers is the number that occurs most frequently.

> In the set {2, 15, 11, 7, 5, 15, 52}, 15 is the mode.

❑ The **range** of a set is the difference between the least and greatest values.

TRY IT OUT

1. What are the median and mode of the following set of numbers?

   {3, 6, 7, 3, 15, 2, 8}

   Median: _____   Mode: _____

2. What are the median and mean of the following set of numbers?

   {18, 11, 12, 10, 19}

   Median: _____   Mean: _____

3. a, b, c, d, and e are consecutive integers appearing in that order.

   Which of the values is equal to the median of the 5 integers?

   Which of the values is equal to the average of the 5 integers?

PUT IT TOGETHER

1. If the average age of a group of 7 friends is 16, which of the following must be true?

   (A) the median age of the group is 16
   (B) if one of the friends is 14, another friend must be 18
   (C) the mode of the group is 9
   (D) the oldest possible age of one of the friends is 32
   (E) the sum of the ages of the friends is 112

   ---

2. In a set with 7 distinct values, the median is 11. The values 9 and 1 are added to the set. Which of the following statements must be true about the new set?

   (A) The median of the set is 11.
   (B) The average of the set is 7.
   (C) The average of the set is 4.
   (D) The median is a value less than 11.
   (E) The median is a value greater than 11.

Sets

❏ A set is a collection of distinct objects, such as a group of numbers or people.

❏ Sets overlap when they have elements in common. Venn diagrams can be used to represent which elements are included in both sets.

> The Venn diagram below shows the numbers 1-12. Set A includes even numbers. Set B contains multiples of 3. The overlapping portion shows even numbers that are also multiples of 3 (6 and 12). Outside of the two sets are the numbers that are odd and are not multiples of 3 (1, 5, 7, and 11).

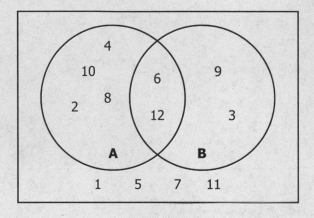

❏ To calculate the total number of elements in a set problem, use the following formula:
Total = Set 1 + Set 2 + Neither − Overlap

> At Tater Industries, 100 employees own cars, 200 own trucks, 50 own both, and 20 own neither. How many employees work at Tater Industries?

PUT IT TOGETHER

1.

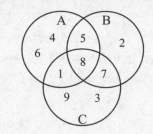

The Venn diagram above shows Set A, Set B, and Set C. Which set represents the intersection of Set A and Set C?

(A) {2}
(B) {1, 8}
(C) {1, 5, 7, 8}
(D) {3, 4, 5, 6, 7, 9}
(E) {1, 3, 4, 5, 6, 7, 8, 9}

_____

2. In the Smithville junior class, 14 students play basketball, 12 play volleyball, and 9 play both basketball and volleyball. If 37 students play neither basketball nor volleyball, how many students are in the Smithville junior class?

(A) 45
(B) 51
(C) 54
(D) 63
(E) 72

Counting

❑ Counting problems involve calculating the total number of choices or outcomes for a situation. Formulas can be used to solve these problems, but many of these problems can also be solved with brute force, listing all of the possibilities and simply counting them.

❑ **Fundamental Principle of Counting** – To determine the total number of different possibilities for a certain situation, multiply the different numbers of possibilities. If there are x options for one choice, and y options for another choice, then there are $x \times y$ combinations of options available.

> If there are 2 candidates for class president and 3 candidates for vice president, how
>
> many different combinations of president/vice president are possible? _____

❑ **Permutations** – In permutations, the order of events matters.

Use the following notations when choosing r items from a set of n items:

$$P(n,r) \quad \text{or} \quad {}_nP_r \quad \text{or} \quad \frac{n!}{(n-r)!}$$

In this formula, **!** denotes a **factorial**. The factorial of n is the product of all positive integers less than or equal to n. For example, $5! = 5 \times 4 \times 3 \times 2 \times 1$.

You may be able to solve permutations similar to how you some simpler counting problems. Determine the number of choices that are made and, one at a time, determine how many options are available for each choice. Then, multiply the numbers of options.

> At a movie theatre, there are 4 friends who are going to sit in a row of 6 seats. How many different ways can the friends arrange themselves in the row?
>
> How many options does the first friend have? _____
>
> How many options does the second friend have? _____
>
> Multiply the numbers of options each friend would have: _____ × _____ × _____ × _____
>
> What is the total number of arrangements? _____

PUT IT TOGETHER

1. Fiona is buying a new car and must choose a car make, model, and trim level. There are 4 makes, which each have 5 different models, and each model has 3 trim levels. How many different options does Fiona have to choose from?

   (A) 60
   (B) 80
   (C) 90
   (D) 120
   (E) 160

2. There are 7 contestants in a cooking contest, and prizes are given to the contestants who receive the highest, second highest, and third highest scores. How many different ways can the 7 contestants finish in first, second, or third place?

   (A) 5040
   (B) 210
   (C) 120
   (D) 24
   (E) 20

Probability

Probability is the likelihood of a certain event occurring.

❑ Probability of an event happening = $\dfrac{\text{\# of ways the event can happen}}{\text{\# of possible outcomes}}$

> In a bag of marbles, there are 2 black marbles, 3 gray marbles, and 4 white marbles. If a marble is chosen randomly from the bag, what are the chances that the marble is black?
>
> Number of black marbles: _____
>
> Total number of marbles: _____
>
> Probability of choosing black: _____

❑ There are different ways to represent probability, including ratios, decimals, and percents. Also, the notation $P(A)$ is used to represent "the probability that A occurs."

> In the dartboard shown below, the gray portions are twice the size of the white portions. If a dart is thrown randomly at the dartboard, what are the odds that it hits a gray part of the board?
>
> Ratio of gray area to white area: _____
>
> Ratio of gray area to total area: _____
>
> Probability of hitting a gray part: _____

❑ **Multiple probabilities** – To find the probability of one event *or* another event occurring, *add* the probabilities of each event. If there is any overlap between the two events, subtract this overlap from the sum.

To find the probability of one event *and* another event occurring, *multiply* the probabilities of each event.

> A coin is flipped 3 times, and every flip results in "heads" or "tails." What are the odds that every flip results in "tails"?
>
> Find the number of possible outcomes: _____
>
> How many outcomes satisfy the description in the question? _____
>
> Create a fraction to represent the probability: _____

TRY IT OUT

1. Jonathan has 3 pennies, 2 nickels, and a quarter in his pocket. If he picks one coin at random, what is the probability that it is a penny?

2. There are 10 male students and 6 female students in a classroom. If one person is chosen at random, what is the probability that it will be a male?

3. A box contains red, white, and blue chips. 18 of the chips are white. 10 of the chips are red. 2 of the chips are blue. What is the probability of NOT drawing a red chip?

4. A deck of cards has 52 different cards. The deck contains 13 card types, including each of the numbers 1-10 and three types of "face" cards (jack, queen, and king). Each type of card has 4 suits (clubs, diamonds, hearts, and spades).

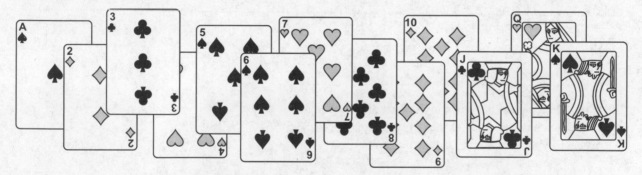

If a card is randomly drawn, what is the probability that it is a face card and a club or spade?

If a card is randomly drawn, what is the probability that it is an even number or a heart?

PUT IT TOGETHER

1. According to the chart, if a brown car is randomly chosen, what are the chances it will be chosen from lot 2?

NUMBER OF CARS OF EACH COLOR
IN THREE LOTS

Car Color	Lot 1	Lot 2	Lot 3
White	12	9	0
Blue	4	0	6
Brown	3	6	1

(A) $\frac{1}{7}$

(B) $\frac{1}{6}$

(C) $\frac{2}{5}$

(D) $\frac{3}{5}$

(E) $\frac{2}{3}$

2. If the 12 men and 20 women in the final drawing for a raffle each have an equal chance of winning, what is the probability that the winner will be a man?

(A) 1 in 2
(B) 1 in 4
(C) 1 in 5
(D) 2 in 5
(E) 3 in 8

3. A market's survey asked whether customers enjoy
    cabbage or spinach. The survey results are in the table
    below.

	Likes Cabbage	Dislikes Cabbage
Likes Spinach	42	24
Dislikes Spinach	60	21

Based on the survey results, if a customer is chosen
randomly, what is the probability that the customer does
not enjoy cabbage or spinach?

(A) 1/7
(B) 1/6
(C) 7/15
(D) 1/2
(E) 7/8

---

4. Events X, Y, and Z are independent and mutually
    exclusive. If $P(X) = 0.5$, $P(Y) = 0.2$, and $P(Z) = 0.3$, what
    is $P(Y$ and $Z)$?

(A) 0.6
(B) 0.5
(C) 0.25
(D) 0.06
(E) 0.05

Interpreting Data

❑ Before looking at a chart or graph question, take a moment to interpret the information presented. Note the title, labels, and units used in graphs and charts. Pay attention to the scale on line graphs and bar graphs, because they might not begin at zero.

❑ Check your answer by reviewing the chart or graph. The figure can help you visualize the information to make sure that your answer makes sense.

❑ Different types of charts and graphs are used to display information. Pay attention to the labels and units.

Favorite Student Activities

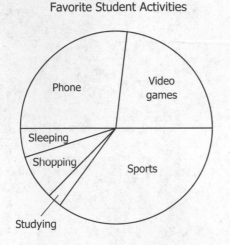

Favorite Student Activities

Activity	Votes
Sports	28
Video games	19
Shopping	6
Sleeping	4
Phone	21
Studying	2

Favorite Student Activities

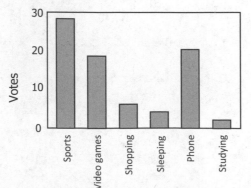

TRY IT OUT

1. How many more rock records than jazz records are there in the collection?

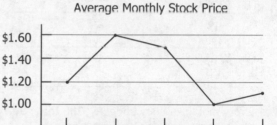

VINYL RECORD COLLECTION
Each ⦿ represents 4 records

Blues	⦿ ⦿ ◖
Jazz	⦿ ⦿ ⦿
Rock	⦿ ⦿ ⦿ ⦿ ◖
Classical	⦿ ◖

2. The number of rock records is how many times the number of classical records?

___

3. According to the graph, what was the average stock price for the 5 months from January to May?

HONEST JOE'S AUTO SHACK
Average Monthly Stock Price

4. According to the graph, in which month was there the greatest change in the average price of the stock compared to the previous month?

___

5. If 50 people saw the film, how many of the viewers were 21 or younger?

AGE DISTRIBUTION OF VIEWERS AT A SCI-FI FILM

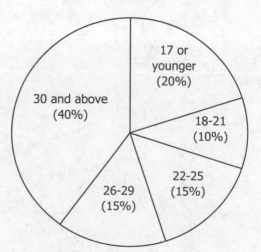

6. If the total number of viewers aged 22-29 was 12, how many viewers saw the film?

PUT IT TOGETHER

Questions 1-2 refer to the graph in Figure 1.

1. According to the chart, the retailer receives how many cents per dollar for food?

   (A) 47.3
   (B) 48.3
   (C) 57.3
   (D) 58.3
   (E) It cannot be determined from the information given.

2. According to the chart, if a farmer earns $1,000 for a shipment of food, which of the following is closest to the amount that the food processors would earn for the shipment?

   (A) $2,000
   (B) $1,800
   (C) $1,600
   (D) $1,400
   (E) $1,000

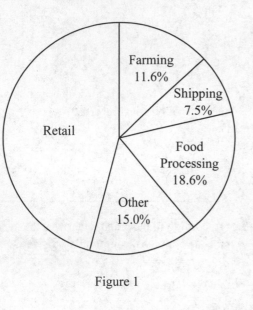

WHERE THE MONEY GOES
WHEN BUYING FOOD

Farming 11.6%
Shipping 7.5%
Retail
Food Processing 18.6%
Other 15.0%

Figure 1

---

3. Every month, Ashley budgets $200 for extra expenses. She spends $100 at restaurants (*R*), $60 on clothing (*C*), and the rest on miscellaneous items (*M*). Which of the following graphs is the best representation of how Ashley budgets her monthly expenses?

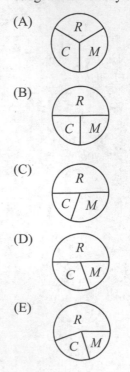

(A)

(B)

(C)

(D)

(E)

Questions 4-6 are based on the graph in Figure 2.

4. The average annual spending on food in 1990 was approximately how much less than in 2000?

    (A) $2,200
    (B) $2,100
    (C) $1,200
    (D) $1,000
    (E) $800

5. The annual expense with the lowest amount in 2010 was how much in 1990?

    (A) $1,200
    (B) $1,400
    (C) $1,600
    (D) $1,800
    (E) $3,200

6. According to the graph, which of the following experienced the greatest increase in annual spending from 2000 to 2010?

    (A) Food
    (B) Shelter
    (C) Health
    (D) Clothing
    (E) Transportation

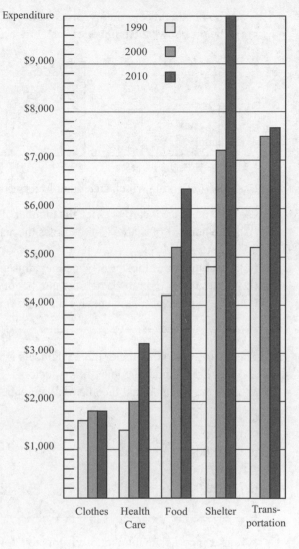

Figure 2

Checkpoint Review

1. A seafood market keeps an inventory of its stock. The graph below shows the number of each product in stock.

    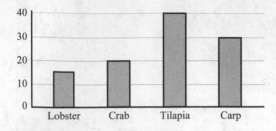

    Based on the graph, which statement is correct?

    (A) The number of carp is twice the number of crabs.
    (B) The number of tilapia is three times the number of lobster.
    (C) The number of lobster is twice the number of carp.
    (D) The number of crabs is half the number of carp.
    (E) The number of tilapia is twice the number of crabs.

    ---

2. The mean annual income of three engineers is $50,000, and the mean annual income of five doctors is $90,000. What is the mean annual income of all eight people?

    (A) $40,000
    (B) $70,000
    (C) $75,000
    (D) $560,000
    (E) $600,000

    ---

3. A ranger records the number of visitors to a park site over a five-day period. The number of park visitors each day is shown in the table below.

Day	Mon	Tue	Wed	Thu	Fri
Visitors	17	19	8	8	18

    Which of the following measures would best represent the anticipated number of park visitors for a random day?

    (A) standard deviation
    (B) median
    (C) mode
    (D) range
    (E) mean

Checkpoint Review

4. In a survey taken of 500 sports fans, 250 fans reported watching baseball and 200 fans reported watching basketball. If half of the fans who watch baseball also watch basketball, how many of the fans reported watching neither baseball nor basketball?

    (A) 50
    (B) 75
    (C) 100
    (D) 125
    (E) 175

5. Tabitha has 3 different softball trophies and 2 different basketball trophies. She wants to arrange the trophies in a row on a shelf so that basketball trophies are on both ends and the softball trophies are in the middle. How many ways can Tabitha arrange her trophies?

    (A) 3
    (B) 8
    (C) 12
    (D) 36
    (E) 60

6. In a gameshow, a contestant spins a wheel and can win three different prizes: A, B, or C. For each spin of the wheel, $P(A) = 0.1$, $P(B) = 0.3$, and $P(C) = 0.6$. If a contestant can spin the wheel twice, what are the odds she does NOT win prize A on either spin?

    (A) 0.01
    (B) 0.20
    (C) 0.36
    (D) 0.81
    (E) 0.99

Chapter Review

❑ Averages

To find the average of a list of numbers, find the sum of the numbers and divide by the number of terms. Average $= \dfrac{\text{sum of parts}}{\text{number of parts}}$

❑ Median, Mode, & Range

The median of a set of numbers is the middle value when all the terms are listed in order according to size. The mode of a set of numbers is the number that occurs most frequently. The range is the difference between the least and greatest values in a set.

❑ Sets

A set is a collection of distinct objects, such as a group of numbers or people. Sets overlap when they have elements in common. Venn diagrams can be used to represent which elements are included in both sets.

❑ Counting

Counting problems involve calculating the total number of choices or outcomes for a situation. Formulas can be used to solve these problems, but many of these problems can also be solved with brute force, listing all of the possibilities and simply counting them.

To determine the total number of different possibilities for a certain situation, multiply the different numbers of possibilities. If there are x options for one choice, and y options for another choice, then there are $x \times y$ combinations of options available.

In permutations, the order of events matters. Use the following notations when choosing r items from a set of n items: $P(n,r)$ or $_nP_r$ or $\dfrac{n!}{(n-r)!}$

❏ Probability

Probability of an event happening $= \dfrac{\text{\# of ways the event can happen}}{\text{\# of possible outcomes}}$

To find the probability of one event *or* another event occurring, *add* the probabilities of each event. If there is any overlap between the two events, subtract this overlap from the sum.

To find the probability of one event *and* another event occurring, *multiply* the probabilities of each event.

❏ Interpreting Data

Before looking at a chart or graph question, take a moment to interpret the information presented. Note the title, labels, and units used in graphs and charts. Pay attention to the scale on line graphs and bar graphs, because they might not begin at zero.

Check your answer by reviewing the chart or graph. The figure can help you visualize the information to make sure that your answer makes sense.

Data Analysis & Probability Practice

Averages

1. The Huskies scored an average of 70 points in their first two games. For the next three games, they averaged 50 points. What was the total number of points scored in those five games?

    (A) 600
    (B) 290
    (C) 240
    (D) 180
    (E) 58

___

2. Among the 3 senior members of a sales team, the average number of clients is 32. Including the 4 junior members, the whole sales team of 7 members has an average of 28 clients. What is the average number of clients among the 4 junior members of the sale team?

    (A) 25
    (B) 26
    (C) 28
    (D) 30
    (E) 34

___

Median, Mode, and Range

3. A data set contains 8 elements and has a mode of 5. Seven of the elements are 2, 3, 5, 5, 6, 6, and 8. Which of the following is the average of the set?

    (A) 3
    (B) 4
    (C) 5
    (D) 6
    (E) 7

4. Given the following list of numbers, which of the statements is true?

    3, 5, 14, 3, 6, –12, 9

    (A) average > median > mode
    (B) mode > median > average
    (C) mode > average > median
    (D) median > average > mode
    (E) median > mode > average

Sets

5. In a book store, 600 books are non-fiction, 900 books are written by female authors, and 460 of the non-fiction books are written by female authors. What is the total number of that store's books that are non-fiction or written by female authors?

    (A) 1040
    (B) 1060
    (C) 1360
    (D) 1500
    (E) 1960

6. Set A is the set of all prime numbers. Set B is the set of all even numbers. Which of the following numbers is included in the intersection between Set A and Set B?

    (A) 1
    (B) 2
    (C) 3
    (D) 4
    (E) 6

Counting

7. A deli offers 4 different types of bread, 3 different meats, 5 different cheeses, and 11 different toppings. If a customer orders a sandwich with 1 type of bread, 2 different types of meat, 1 type of cheese, and 2 different toppings, how many different sandwich combinations are possible?

    (A) 35
    (B) 37
    (C) 264
    (D) 13,200
    (E) 21,780

Probability

8. In a class of 30 students, 18 are female and 12 are male. If a student is chosen at random to be a teacher's assistant, what is the probability that a female is chosen?

    (A) $\dfrac{1}{5}$

    (B) $\dfrac{1}{3}$

    (C) $\dfrac{2}{5}$

    (D) $\dfrac{3}{5}$

    (E) $\dfrac{2}{3}$

Interpreting Data

Questions 9 and 10 relate to the chart below.

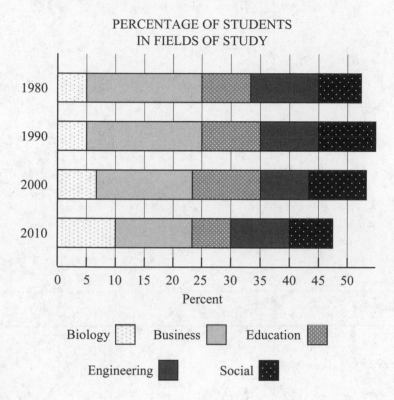

PERCENTAGE OF STUDENTS
IN FIELDS OF STUDY

9. In which category was the percent of students enrolled in
    1990 most nearly equal to the percent of students enrolled
    in 2010?

    (A) Biology
    (B) Business
    (C) Education
    (D) Engineering
    (E) Social Science

10. The percent of students studying business in 1980 was
    approximately how many times the percent of students
    studying education in 2010?

    (A) 2
    (B) 3
    (C) 4
    (D) 5
    (E) 13

Data Analysis & Probability Practice – Middle Level

1. The average age of the 10 members of the basketball team is 28. The average age of the 30 members of the sewing club is 60. What is the average age of all the members of the basketball team and the sewing club?

    (A) 56
    (B) 52
    (C) 50
    (D) 48
    (E) 46

2. A website tracks the number of page views of an article for one week. The number of page views are displayed in the table shown below.

Day	Sun	Mon	Tue	Wed	Thu	Fri	Sat
Views	97	83	41	8	21	164	111

    Based on the data shown, what was the average daily number of page views?

    (A) 65
    (B) 75
    (C) 85
    (D) 95
    (E) 105

3. Three people buying a present together each pay $10. How much would each person pay if a fourth person shared the cost of the present?

    (A) $2.50
    (B) $3.00
    (C) $6.00
    (D) $7.50
    (E) $9.00

SUMMIT
EDUCATIONAL
GROUP

4.

Number of students	Score
3	100
0	90
2	80
1	70
4	60
1	50

The table above shows the scores for 11 students on a vocabulary quiz. Two more student's scores are added to the table, and the median score does not change. If one of the added scores is 60, what must be true of the other added score?

(A) The score is 80.
(B) The score is 80 or higher.
(C) The score is 70 or lower.
(D) The score is 70 or higher.
(E) The score is lower than 80.

5. If the first number picked in a BINGO game is odd, which of the following rows is most likely to have that number?

(A) 2   4   8   7   6
(B) 11 19 18 12 13
(C) 21 24 30 27 24
(D) 31 38 37 33 35
(E) 42 40 46 44 48

6. After four tests, Kevin had an average of 77 points per test. After the fifth test, his average was 80 points per test. How many points did Kevin score on the fifth test?

(A) 98
(B) 92
(C) 89
(D) 78
(E) 72

7. The line graph shows the population of buffalo within a nature reserve over a 50-year period.

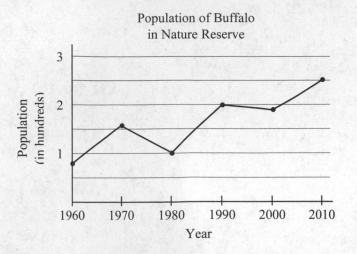

Population of Buffalo
in Nature Reserve

Which of the following is the approximate difference in population from 1980 to 2000?

(A) 1
(B) 90
(C) 110
(D) 180
(E) 220

8. There are 22 students in a class and 14 of them are female. If 16 of the students have brown eyes, and if 3 of the male students do not have brown eyes, what is the total number of female students with brown eyes in the class?

(A) 3
(B) 9
(C) 11
(D) 13
(E) 17

9. The composition of air, by volume, is detailed in the graph below.

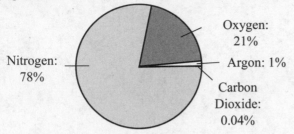

    According to the chart, if a volume of air contains 1 cubic centimeter of carbon dioxide, it will contain how much oxygen, in cubic centimeters?

    (A) 25
    (B) 84
    (C) 420
    (D) 525
    (E) 2096

10. The probability of randomly choosing a red marble from a bag is between 0 and 1/3. If there are only red and white marbles in the bag and 10 of the marbles are red, which of the following could be the number of white marbles in the bag?

    (A) 4
    (B) 6
    (C) 10
    (D) 15
    (E) 22

Data Analysis & Probability Practice – Upper Level

1. Set A = {1, 4, 9, 13}
    Set B = {2, 3, 4, 8, 9, 18}
    Set C = {9, 12, 15, 18, 21}

    What is the intersection of Set A, Set B, and Set C?

    (A) {1, 2, 3, 4, 7, 8, 9, 12, 13, 15, 18, 21}
    (B) {1, 2, 3, 7, 8, 12, 13, 15, 21}
    (C) {4, 9, 18}
    (D) {4, 18}
    (E) {9}

2. Edna rolls three 6-sided dice. Each side of the dice has a number 1 through 6, and no two side of the same dice share the same number. What are the odds that Edna rolls three odd numbers?

    (A) $\dfrac{1}{2}$

    (B) $\dfrac{1}{4}$

    (C) $\dfrac{1}{6}$

    (D) $\dfrac{1}{8}$

    (E) $\dfrac{1}{18}$

3. Garth bicycles a distance of 30 miles in 5 hours. He stops for 2 hours to rest and do repairs on his bicycle. Then he bicycles another 50 miles in 3 hours. What is Garth's average speed, in miles per hour, for his entire trip?

    (A) 40
    (B) 20
    (C) 13
    (D) 10
    (E) 8

4.

From the shapes shown above, 3 shapes are chosen. If no shape can be chosen more than once, how many different combinations of 3 shapes can be chosen?

(A) 12
(B) 16
(C) 20
(D) 60
(E) 120

5. What is the intersection of the set of prime numbers and the set of even integers?

(A) {2}
(B) {-2, 2}
(C) {0, 1, 2}
(D) {0, 2, 4}
(E) There is no number that is both prime and even.

6. There are 30 wrapped prizes in a bag. 12 of the prizes are toys, 6 are candy, 4 are gift certificates, and the rest are books. If Jessica takes a prize without looking in the bag, what are her chances of choosing a book?

(A) 2 in 15
(B) 1 in 5
(C) 4 in 15
(D) 1 in 4
(E) 1 in 3

7. A weather forecast states the probability of snow on Saturday is 0.7 and the probability of snow on Sunday is 0.3. According to the forecast, if the weather on Saturday does not affect the forecast for Sunday, what is the likelihood that it does not snow on Saturday and does snow on Sunday?

(A) 0.09
(B) 0.21
(C) 0.31
(D) 0.4
(E) 1.0

8. Four people have spent an average of $9 each in supplies
    for a class project. If they contribute a total of $7 more for
    supplies to complete the project, how many dollars in all
    will be spent on the project?

    (A) $64
    (B) $63
    (C) $54
    (D) $44
    (E) $43

9. In a class of 40 students, 25 take home economics and 25
    take woodworking. If everyone in the class takes either
    home economics, woodworking, or both, how many take
    both?

    (A) 5
    (B) 10
    (C) 15
    (D) 20
    (E) 25

10. If the average of two numbers is 20, which of the
    following statements must be true?

    I.   If one of the two numbers is 11, the other number is
         less than 30.
    II. If a third number is added and the average jumps to
         25, the third number is greater than 30.
    III. If each of the two numbers is reduced by 2, the
         average is reduced by 4.

    (A) I only
    (B) II only
    (C) III only
    (D) I and II only
    (E) I,II, and III

SUMMIT
EDUCATIONAL
GROUP

Answer Key

TEST-TAKING FUNDAMENTALS

Pg. 8 – BEATING THE SSAT

Try It Out

1. correct answer: D. attractor: B

Pg. 10 – MAKING YOUR BEST GUESS

D

Pg. 12 – USING THE ANSWER CHOICES

Try It Out

1. B

QUANTITATIVE

Pg. 20 – PLUGGING IN

Put It Together

1. D
2. C
3. E
4. A

Pg. 22 – SOLVING BACKWARDS

Put It Together

1. E
2. B
3. A

Pg. 24 – CHOOSING NUMBERS

Put It Together

1. A
2. D
3. D

NUMBER CONCEPTS & OPERATIONS

Pg. 32 – ADDITION, SUBTRACTION, MULTIPLICATION, & DIVISION

0
0
2, 345
999
1
9,300
63,400
2.6
24.35

Try It Out

1. 100,700
2. 11,000
3. 1,150
4. 6,020
5. 11,110
6. 3,813
7. 0
8. 1,000
9. 13,000
10. 85
11. 21
12. 621
13. 28,900
14. 0
15. 999.9
16. 22
17. 412
18. 0
19. 347.76
20. 1

Put It Together

1. B
2. B
3. B
4. C
5. C
6. B
7. D

Pg. 36 – ODD & EVEN INTEGERS

Try It Out

1. 4, 6, 400
2. 0, 12, 18, 100
3. 1, 3, 11, 21

Put It Together

1. C
2. E
3. D

Pg. 38 – POSITIVE & NEGATIVE NUMBERS

-5
5
3
-48

Try It Out

1. −3
2. 1
3. 7
4. 0
5. 1
6. −1
7. −12
8. −5
9. 23
10. −4
11. 8
12. −15
13. −10
14. 12
15. 4

Put It Together

1. A
2. E

Pg. 40 – DIVISIBILITY & REMAINDERS

Try It Out

1. yes
2. no
3. 2
4. 0
5. 7

Put It Together

1. B
2. E
3. D

Pg. 42 – MULTIPLES AND FACTORS

Try It Out

1. 1, 32, 2, 16, 4, 8
2. 1, 63, 3, 21, 7, 9
3. 2, 4, 6, 8, 10
4. 12, 24, 36
5. 2, 2, 2, 3   2, 2, 3, 7   2, 2, 5, 5

Put It Together

1. E
2. E
3. D

Pg. 44 – CHECKPOINT REVIEW

1. D
2. A
3. C
4. C
5. E
6. C
7. A
8. E

Pg. 46 – FRACTIONS

$2 + \dfrac{5}{6}$

$\dfrac{19}{4}$

$6\dfrac{2}{3}$

Try It Out

1. $\dfrac{5}{1}$

2. $\dfrac{20}{3}$

3. $\dfrac{41}{7}$

4. $1\dfrac{1}{2}$

5. $2\dfrac{2}{3}$

6. $4\dfrac{3}{4}$

7. 10
8. 12
9. 14
10. 5
11. 70
12. 450

Put It Together

1. E
2. D
3. C
4. B
5. B
6. E
7. D
8. D

Pg. 50 – REDUCING FRACTIONS

Try It Out

1. $\frac{2}{3}$

2. $\frac{13}{15}$

3. $\frac{9}{20}$

4. $\frac{4}{9}$

5. $\frac{1}{3}, \frac{3}{8}, \frac{4}{3}$

6. $\frac{3}{8}, \frac{2}{5}, \frac{3}{4}$

7. $\frac{1}{6}, \frac{7}{30}, \frac{8}{15}, \frac{4}{5}$

8. $\frac{3}{7}, \frac{1}{2}, \frac{2}{3}, \frac{4}{5}$

Put It Together

1. B
2. C
3. A
4. E

Pg. 54 – ADDING & SUBTRACTING FRACTIONS

Try It Out

1. $\frac{2}{3}$

2. $\frac{5}{6}$

3. $\frac{2}{3}$

4. $\frac{3}{4}$

5. $1\frac{2}{15}$

6. $\frac{17}{18}$

7. $1\frac{1}{2}$

8. $7\frac{5}{6}$

9. $\frac{1}{3}$

10. $\frac{1}{4}$

11. $\frac{3}{10}$

12. $\frac{1}{12}$

13. $\frac{5}{14}$

14. $6\frac{2}{3}$

15. 1

16. $1\frac{1}{2}$

17. $2\frac{2}{5}$

Put It Together

1. E
2. D
3. E
4. A
5. B
6. E

Pg. 58 – MULTIPLYING & DIVIDING FRACTIONS

Try It Out

1. $\frac{2}{21}$

2. $\frac{1}{5}$

3. $\frac{2}{5}$

4. $\frac{2}{5}$

5. $\frac{2}{5}$

6. 12

7. $4\frac{1}{6}$

8. 21

9. $1\frac{1}{2}$

10. 2

11. $\frac{4}{5}$

12. $\frac{2}{3}$

13. $5\frac{1}{5}$

14. 4
15. 30
16. 49

Put It Together

1. B
2. E
3. D
4. E
5. A
6. B

Pg. 62 – CHECKPOINT REVIEW

1. D
2. D
3. E
4. E
5. C
6. C

Pg. 64 –PLACE VALUE

1200/10,000 = 0.12

Try It Out

1. 8
2. 5

Put It Together

1. C
2. D
3. D
4. B

Pg. 66 – ROUNDING & ESTIMATION

Try It Out

1. 2
2. 1.5
3. 2.23
4. 23
5. 400
6. 350
7. 100.0
8. D
9. C

Put It Together

1. B
2. A
3. D
4. E
5. B

Pg. 70 – DECIMALS

Try It Out

1. 18.8203
2. 83
3. 7.65
4. 96.55
5. 0.95
6. 25.29
7. 0.98
8. 0.0042
9. 2,900
10. 3.294

11. 90
12. 40
13. 40
14. 2.01
15. 160
16. 30.2

Put It Together

1. C
2. D

Pg. 72 – PERCENT-DECIMAL-FRACTION CONVERSION

Try It Out

1. 63%
2. 207%
3. 4%
4. 12.56%
5. 0.05%
6. 0.73
7. 1.19
8. 0.075
9. 0.0075
10. 0.021
11. $\dfrac{2}{5}$
12. $\dfrac{17}{25}$
13. $\dfrac{2}{25}$
14. $1\dfrac{2}{5}$
15. $10\dfrac{1}{100}$
16. 10%
17. 25%
18. 60%
19. 120%
20. 71%

Put It Together

1. E
2. B
3. B
4. A

Pg. 76 —PERCENTS

Try It Out

1. 4.8
2. 62.5
3. 1.28
4. 45
5. 50
6. 75
7. 125
8. 33.$\overline{3}$
9. 200
10. 6.25
11. 30
12. 2

Put It Together

1. C
2. E
3. C
4. B
5. C
6. A
7. D

Pg. 80 – CHECKPOINT REVIEW

1. B
2. C
3. D
4. E
5. C
6. C
7. D

Pg. 82 – RATIOS

Try It Out

1. 4:7
2. 2:5
3. 5:18
4. 3:2
5. 10
6. 12
7. 30

Put It Together

1. A
2. A
3. B
4. C
5. B
6. D

Pg. 86 – PROPORTIONS

Try It Out

1. 8
2. 10
3. 12
4. 16
5. $8\frac{1}{3}$
6. $450
7. 60
8. 25 miles
9. 4

Put It Together

1. A
2. B
3. C
4. A

Pg. 90 – ORDER OF OPERATIONS

Try It Out

1. 37
2. 7
3. 196
4. 1

Put It Together

1. D
2. A

Pg. 92 —SEQUENCES, PATTERNS, & LOGIC

Try It Out

1. 33.1, 33.01, 4.23, 4.1937, .00936
2. $\frac{7}{10}$, $\frac{2}{3}$, $\frac{3}{5}$, $\frac{5}{12}$
3. Fred
4. 19

Put It Together

1. E
2. B
3. A
4. B
5. C

Pg. 96 – CHECKPOINT REVIEW

1. C
2. B
3. C
4. E
5. B

NUMBER CONCEPTS & OPERATIONS PRACTICE

Pg. 100

1. E
2. B
3. B
4. E
5. C
6. D
7. C
8. E
9. C
10. B
11. A
12. C
13. B
14. D
15. B
16. E
17. E
18. A
19. A
20. C
21. D
22. C
23. C
24. B
25. A
26. D
27. A
28. A
29. D
30. B
31. B
32. C
33. C
34. D
35. E
36. D
37. D
38. E
39. D
40. B
41. C
42. A
43. E
44. C
45. B
46. B
47. B
48. C
49. A
50. D
51. C
52. C
53. B

54. A
55. D

NUMBER CONCEPTS & OPERATIONS PRACTICE – MIDDLE LEVEL

Pg. 114

1. D
2. B
3. D
4. A
5. D
6. B
7. D
8. D
9. D
10. B
11. E
12. E
13. B
14. A
15. A
16. C
17. E
18. D
19. E
20. E
21. C
22. D
23. A
24. C
25. A
26. C
27. C
28. E
29. B
30. C
31. E
32. B
33. C
34. A
35. D
36. D
37. D
38. D
39. D
40. D
41. A
42. B
43. D
44. A
45. B
46. B
47. B
48. B
49. A
50. A

NUMBER CONCEPTS & OPERATIONS
PRACTICE – UPPER LEVEL

Pg. 128

1. B
2. C
3. E
4. A
5. C
6. A
7. D
8. C
9. D
10. D
11. C
12. C
13. C
14. A
15. D
16. D
17. A
18. C
19. D
20. E
21. D
22. C
23. A
24. C
25. E
26. E
27. D
28. D
29. C
30. C
31. D
32. D
33. B
34. B
35. C
36. A
37. A
38. D
39. D
40. D
41. C
42. E
43. D
44. C
45. E
46. E
47. D
48. C
49. A
50. B

ALGEBRA

Pg. 146 – ABSOLUTE VALUE

$$|7(-3)+4(5)|=1$$
$$|5-3|-|6-9|=-1$$

Try It Out

1. 7
2. 10
3. 6
4. 6
5. -4
6. -2

Put It Together

1. B
2. C
3. B

Pg. 148 – SCIENTIFIC NOTATION

6.78×10^{-13}
8,630,000

Put It Together

1. A
2. D

Pg. 150 – EXPONENTS

$21^0 = 1$
$100^1 = 100$
$3^3 = 27$
$$\left(\frac{2}{3}\right)^2 = \frac{4}{9}$$
$$\left(\frac{1}{3}\right)^4 = \frac{1}{81}$$
$(-4)^2 = 16$
$(-2)^3 = -8$

Try It Out

1. 1
2. 2
3. 8
4. 4
5. -8
6. 16
7. 1
8. −1
9. $\frac{1}{9}$
10. $\frac{8}{27}$
11. 3 or −3

12. 4
13. −2
14. −1
15. $\dfrac{1}{10}$
16. 3

Put It Together

1. D
2. D

Pg. 85 – MULTIPLYING & DIVIDING NUMBERS WITH EXPONENTS

$t \times t^4 = t^5$

$\dfrac{b^6}{b^5} = b$

$\left(2^3\right)^7 = 2^{21}$

$\left(d^3\right)^5 = d^{15}$

Try It Out

1. 2^5 or 32
2. x^7
3. 7
4. x^{10}
5. 6^6
6. x^{44}
7. $16x^6$

Put It Together

1. E
2. A

Pg. 87 – ROOTS

Try It Out

1. 4
2. 7
3. $\dfrac{1}{3}$
4. $\dfrac{2}{3}$
5. x
6. x^2
7. $2x^5$
8. 10
9. 4
10. −1
11. −5
12. $\dfrac{1}{2}$
13. $2\sqrt{2}$
14. $2\sqrt{3}$

15. $4\sqrt{5}$
16. $4\sqrt{2}$

Put It Together

1. D
2. C

Pg. 156 – CHECKPOINT REVIEW

1. E
2. D
3. C
4. A
5. D
6. B
7. B
8. A

Pg. 158 – ALGEBRAIC EXPRESSIONS

$(3y + 6)(y - 5) = 3y^2 - 9y - 30$

Try It Out

1. $17 + 3x$
2. $12 + x$
3. $-4x$
4. $3x^2 + 3$
5. $-3x^2 + 5x + 12$
6. $3x + 10$
7. $x + 1$
8. $3x + 1$
9. $-14x + 7$
10. $2x + 6$
11. $8x + 28$
12. $-4x - 3$
13. $-3x - 18$
14. $35x - 42$
15. $x^2 + x$
16. $2x^2 - 12x$
17. $-5x^2 - 20x$
18. $8x^2 + 18x$
19. $22x + 2$
20. $5x^2 - 12x - 14$

Put It Together

1. A
2. A
3. D
4. B
5. C
6. B

Pg. 162 – ALGEBRAIC EQUATIONS

$x + 4 = -7$
$x = 6$
$\sqrt{x} = 8 - 1$
$x = 49$

Try It Out

1. 11
2. 5
3. 0
4. 1000
5. 50
6. 1
7. 20
8. 125
9. 10
10. 20
11. 60
12. 12
13. 4
14. 100
15. 18
16. 11.25
17. 16
18. 98
19. 4
20. 8

Put It Together

1. D
2. D
3. D
4. E
5. A
6. C
7. D
8. E

Pg. 166 – INEQUALITIES

$6 < N < 11$
7, 9, 11, 13, 15, 17, 19

Try It Out

1. 3, 4
2. 1, 3, 5, 7
3. -2, -1
4. $n > 4$
5. $x \leq 18$
6. $x < 2$
7. $s \geq 1\frac{1}{2}$
8. $x < -4$
9. $r > -3$
10. $m < 3$

Put It Together

1. D
2. E
3. C
4. E
5. D
6. E

Pg. 170 – SIMULTANEOUS EQUATIONS

Multiply by 2
$x = 7$
$y = 3 - 2x$
$x = 3$
$C =$ number of children tickets
$10A + 2C - 5200$
$A = 400$

Put It Together

1. A
2. B
3. D

Pg. 172 – CHECKPOINT REVIEW

1. C
2. B
3. B
4. C
5. A
6. A

Pg. 174 – TRANSLATING

Try It Out

1. $\frac{50}{100} \cdot (24) = x$, $x = 12$
2. $y - 6 = 17$, $y = 23$
3. $\frac{1}{2} \cdot (28) = x$, $x = 14$
4. $9 + u = a$
5. $1 + z = x$
6. $u + v + w = 9$
7. $7 \times 4 = y$, $y = 28$
8. $-5 = \frac{a + b + c}{3}$
9. $S = F - 2$
10. $2N + 1 = 11$, $N = 5$
11. 9
12. 54
13. 10
14. 11
15. 13

Put It Together

1. B
2. D
3. D
4. D
5. C
6. A
7. A

Pg. 178 – FUNCTIONS

$f(1) = 1$
$f(t) = -3t - 2$
$a = 17$

Try It Out

1. 3
2. 28
3. -4

Put It Together

1. E
2. C
3. E

Pg. 180 – SSAT FUNCTIONS

Try It Out

1. C
2. B
3. C
4. C
5. A

Put It Together

1. C
2. D
3. B
4. B
5. D
6. E

Pg. 184 – QUADRATIC EQUATIONS

$(x^2 + 7x + 10) = (x + 5)(x + 2)$
$x = -1, -7$
$x^2 - 16 = (x + 4)(x - 4)$

Try It Out

1. $(x + 2)(x + 3)$
2. $(x - 7)(x + 3)$
3. $(2x + 1)(x + 2)$
4. 3, 2
5. 3, -4
6. -1, -2

Put It Together

1. C
2. B
3. D
4. C

Pg. 186 – CHECKPOINT REVIEW

1. B
2. A
3. D
4. B
5. E
6. E
7. C
8. E

ALGEBRA PRACTICE

Pg. 190

1. A
2. C
3. D
4. A
5. B
6. C
7. E
8. D
9. C
10. D
11. A
12. B
13. B
14. D
15. D
16. C
17. E
18. A
19. D
20. E
21. E
22. E
23. C
24. D
25. B
26. C
27. D
28. E
29. E
30. D
31. A
32. E
33. C
34. D
35. B
36. C
37. D
38. A
39. A
40. E

ALGEBRA PRACTICE – MIDDLE LEVEL

Pg. 200

1. C
2. E
3. C
4. C
5. D
6. C
7. B
8. D
9. C
10. B
11. B
12. C
13. C
14. D
15. C
16. D
17. D
18. E
19. D
20. D
21. D
22. C
23. B
24. C
25. C

ALGEBRA PRACTICE – UPPER LEVEL

Pg. 206

1. B
2. E
3. E
4. B
5. B
6. C
7. E
8. C
9. B
10. D
11. E
12. E
13. A
14. C
15. B
16. E
17. E
18. B
19. C
20. E
21. D
22. B
23. E
24. E
25. A

GEOMETRY

Pg. 216 – ANGLES

$a + b + c + d = 360°$
$a = c, b = d$
$x + y + z = 180°$
$a + b + c + d = 360°$
$a + b + c + d + e = 540°$
$a = 108°$

Try It Out

1. ~45°
2. ~80°
3. ~150°
4. 90°
5. 120°
6. 150°
7. ~50° and ~40° (sum is 90°)
8. 60°
9. 145°
10. 45°
11. 75°
12. 55°

Put It Together

1. A
2. C
3. D
4. A

Pg. 220 – PARALLEL LINES

Try It Out

Angles are 30° and 150°

Put It Together

1. D
2. D

Pg. 222 – ISOSCELES & EQUILATERAL TRIANGLES

Try It Out

1. 45° and 45°
2. 46° and 46°

Put It Together

1. B
2. C

Pg. 224 – RIGHT TRIANGLES

Try It Out

1. Sum of all angles in a triangle is 180°. The sum of the two non-right angles must be 90° so that the sum of these angles and the right angle will be 180°.
2. 60°

Put It Together

1. A
2. C

Pg. 226 – CHECKPOINT REVIEW

1. C
2. A
3. C
4. B
5. B
6. B

Pg. 228 – AREA & PERIMETER – RECTANGLE & SQUARE

Try It Out

1. Perimeter = 8, Area = 4
2. Area = 21, Perimeter = 20

Put It Together

1. D
2. B
3. E
4. C
5. A
6. E

Pg. 232 – AREA & PERIMETER – TRIANGLE

Try It Out

1. 12
2. 6
3. 6
4. 7.5
5. 3

Put It Together

1. B
2. D
3. C
4. B
5. A

Pg. 236 – CIRCLES

Try It Out

1. 8π
2. 6π
3. 16π
4. 9π

Put It Together

1. C
2. C
3. C
4. D

Pg. 240 – VOLUME

Try It Out

1. 64
2. 48

Put It Together

1. C
2. A

Pg. 242 – SPATIAL REASONING

D

Put It Together

1. C
2. D

Pg. 244 – CHECKPOINT REVIEW

1. E
2. C
3. B
4. C

Pg. 246 – COORDINATE PLANE

Try It Out

1.

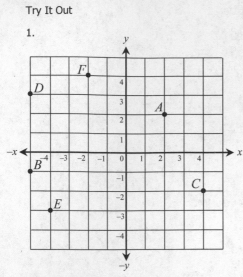

2.   K: (0, 4)
     L: (2, 3)
     M: (4, 2)
     N: (−1, 1)
     P: (3, 0)
     Q: (−3, −2)
     R: (−1, −2)
     S: (2, −2)

Put It Together

1.   A
2.   D

Pg. 248 – MIDPOINT & DISTANCE

Try It Out

1.   (2,0)
2.   (1.5, 0.5)
3.   2√2
4.   √61

Put It Together

1.   D
2.   C

Pg. 250 – TRANSFORMATIONS

Put It Together

1.   B
2.   C
3.   D

Pg. 252 – SLOPE

1
-1/3
-1/2

Try It Out

1.   1
2.   3
3.   -3
4. $\frac{2}{3}$
5. $-\frac{1}{3}$
6.   S
7.   T

Put It Together

1.   C
2.   A

Pg. 254 – GRAPHING LINES

Try It Out

1.

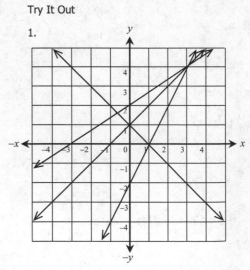

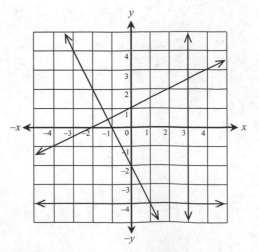

2. A: $x = -4$
    B: $y = x - 3$
    C: $y = \frac{1}{2}x - 2$
    D: $y = -x + 4$
    E: $y = -2x + 2$
3. $y = x + 4$
4. $y = -3x + 2$
5. $y = -\frac{2}{3}x - 1$

Put It Together

1. B
2. A
3. C

Pg. 258 – CHECKPOINT REVIEW

1. B
2. E
3. C
4. E

GEOMETRY PRACTICE

Pg. 262

1. B
2. D
3. B
4. C
5. C
6. D
7. A
8. C
9. C
10. C
11. C
12. A
13. D
14. C
15. E
16. E
17. C
18. A
19. A
20. E
21. D
22. B
23. E
24. D
25. C

GEOMETRY PRACTICE – MIDDLE LEVEL

Pg. 272

1. D
2. E
3. A
4. C
5. D
6. C
7. C
8. A
9. C
10. B
11. D
12. C
13. C
14. D
15. D
16. E
17. A
18. A
19. D
20. C
21. C
22. B
23. C
24. C
25. A

GEOMETRY PRACTICE – UPPER LEVEL

Pg. 282

1. D
2. E
3. C
4. D
5. B
6. C
7. C
8. E
9. B
10. E
11. C
12. B
13. D
14. E
15. E
16. D
17. D
18. D
19. B
20. B
21. B
22. A
23. D
24. D
25. B

DATA ANALYSIS & PROBABILITY

Pg. 294 – AVERAGES

Try It Out

1. 16
2. 100
3. 9
4. 39
5. 5
6. 2
7. 18
8. 52
9. $170
10. 11

Put It Together

1. B
2. D
3. C
4. E

Pg. 298 – MEDIAN, MODE, & RANGE

Try It Out

1. 6, 3
2. 12, 14
3. C, C

Put It Together

1. E
2. D

Pg. 300 – SETS

100 + 200 + 20 − 50 = 270 employees

Put It Together

1. B
2. C

Pg. 302 – COUNTING

6 combinations of president and vice president
first friend = 6
second friend = 5
6 × 5 × 4 × 3 = 360 arrangements

Put It Together

1. A
2. B

Pg. 304 – PROBABILITY

black marbles = 2
total marbles = 9
probability = 2/9
gray/white = 2/1
gray/total = 2/3
probability = 2/3
outcomes = HHH HHT HTH HTT THH THT TTH TTT
probability = 1/8

Try It Out

1. $\frac{1}{2}$
2. $\frac{5}{8}$
3. $\frac{2}{3}$
4. $\frac{3}{26}$

There are 13 heart cards and 20 even cards. However, 5 of the number cards are heart cards. So, there are 20 + 13 − 5 = 28 cards that are an even or heart. The odds of are 28/52 or 7/13.

Put It Together

1. D
2. E
3. A
4. D

Pg. 308 – INTERPRETING DATA

Try It Out

1. 6
2. 3
3. $1.28
4. March to April
5. 15
6. 40

Put It Together

1. A
2. C
3. D
4. D
5. C
6. B

Pg. 312 – CHECKPOINT REVIEW

1. E
2. C
3. E
4. E
5. C
6. D

DATA ANALYSIS & PROBABILITY PRACTICE

Pg. 316

1. B
2. A
3. C
4. D
5. A
6. B
7. D
8. D
9. D
10. B

DATA ANALYSIS & PROBABILITY PRACTICE – MIDDLE LEVEL

Pg. 320

1. B
2. B
3. D
4. D
5. D
6. B
7. B
8. C
9. D
10. E

DATA ANALYSIS & PROBABILITY PRACTICE – UPPER LEVEL

Pg. 324

1. E
2. D
3. E
4. D
5. A
6. C
7. A
8. E
9. B
10. D